PAPPY

THE GENTLE BEAR

oach Who Changed Football...
AND the Men Who Played It

PAPPY

THE GENTLE BEAR

oACH WHO CHANGED FOOTBALL...
AND THE MEN WHO PLAYED IT

ADDAX
PUBLISHING
GROUP

Lenexa, KS

Published by Addax Publishing Group, Inc.

Copyright © 2000 by Steve Cameron & John Greenburg

Edited by Judy Widener

Designed by Randy Breeden

Cover Designed by Laura Bolter

For information address:
Addax Publishing Group, Inc.
8643 Hauser Drive, Suite 235, Lenexa, KS 66215

ISBN: 1-886110-80-8

Printed in the USA

1 3 5 7 9 10 8 6 4 2

ATTENTION: SCHOOLS AND BUSINESSES

Addax Publishing Group, Inc. books are available at quantity discounts with bulk purchase for education, business, or sales promotional use. For information, please write to: Special Sales Department, Addax Publishing Group, Inc., 8643 Hauser Drive, Suite 235, Lenexa, Kansas 66215.

Library of Congress Cataloging-in-Publication Data

Cameron, Steve.
    Pappy, the gentle bear : a coach who changed football, and the men who played it /
by
    Steve Cameron and John Greenburg ; foreword by Bill Walsh.
        p. cm.
    ISBN: 1-8861110-80-8
    1. Waldorf, Lynn O., 1902-1981. 2. Football coaches—United States—Biography. 3.
University of California, Berkeley—Football—History. I. Greenburg, John. II. Title.

GV939.W23 C26 2000
796.332'092—dc21
[B]
                                                                        99-051514

DEDICATION

For my own family, as always, and for the huge family of people who were touched by the greatness of Pappy Waldorf.

—S.C.

I dedicate this book to all football coaches — past, present and future. Thank God for your hardy breed. You build men by teaching a humbling game, and in the process make the days so interesting for so many of us.

—J. G.

TABLE OF CONTENTS

ACKNOWLEDGMENTS

I t would be impossible to list everyone who helped put this project together.

Yes, most authors say that whenever a book is finished, but in this case, those words ring true. So many people who knew and loved Pappy Waldorf took the time to help, contribute pictures, or share memories, that it truly boggles the mind.

However, I would be remiss not to single out a few folks who went beyond the call: Roy Muehlberger, whose passion got this book written, pure and simple; Dick and Jan Erickson, who kept the pot bubbling and opened so many doors; and the two Waldorf girls, Mary Louise Osborne and Carolyn Pickering, who answered every call and lent some photographs that add something very special to the finished product.

Speaking of the photos, longtime Berkeley graphics genius Ed Kirwin deserves a bow, and thanks also to Marty Cullom, Boots Erb and everyone else who offered more pictures than could be used.

Another fellow who deserves a mention is *Sports Illustrated* senior writer Ron Fimrite. A loyal Old Blue in his own right, Ron edited that great book, "Pappy's Boys," which members of that organization had published for their own satisfaction, and from which we have drawn tons of material.

Thanks, also, to everyone at Addax Publishing Group for believing in this project and hanging tough. Bob Snodgrass and Darcie Kidson deserve medals, and Darcie should get a Purple Heart for taking so many hits right on deadline.

Staff and supporters at the University of California, Northwestern University and several other fine institutions also contributed to this effort, and naturally material has been borrowed from magazines and newspaper accounts by the hundreds.

Also, it would be folly not to mention Roy Muehlberger's lovely wife, Nancy. It just would.

See, getting all the proper acknowledgments into print really is too much — at least on a project like this one.

Maybe I should just thank Pappy Waldorf and be done. After all, he's the guy whose soul appears on every page.

God bless you, Pappy.

-Steve Cameron

ACKNOWLEDGMENTS

To write this book meant contacting hundreds of men and women all over the country who had played for or known Coach Waldorf. Each person was most considerate, generous with their time and willing to share their memories. Each of them has my gratitude. I couldn't have done this project without them.

In addition, I must give special mention to nine people — a true "major league nine" — who played vital roles in my what I have accomplished. First, to Bob Snodgrass: Thanks for giving me a chance to show what I could do. To Ed Burtis and his son Dan: Thanks for supporting and sustaining me, for giving good advice, but, especially, for respecting what I was committed to. To Wayne and Louise Holmes, Oklahomans who became Californians: Thanks for your hospitality when I went to the West Coast, and for being there for me all these years. To Tom Smusyn, Ellen Herdeck, Erick Field and Julie Webb: Thanks for being interested during all that time when very few people seemed to care.

-John Greenburg

11

Foreword

By Bill Walsh

Vice President/General Manager

San Francisco 49ers

When college football was the premier sport in the country, Pappy Waldorf headed the list of truly great coaches who had longevity and continued success.

He basically changed the picture on the West Coast when he arrived at the University of California. West Coast football previously had been dominated by USC, to some extent by Washington and occasionally UCLA, but Pappy Waldorf brought great, top-flight football to the western part of the United States when he came to Berkeley. With Coach Waldorf, highly-ranked teams were the norm. Cal was not an easy place for a coach to thrive, either, because admissions requirements were higher than those of many competing universities. Pappy had to work with the kind of men who could qualify at Cal and also compete at the highest level.

He came within inches of winning Rose Bowl games playing

against the best teams in football. There wasn't any question that his opponents and Cal were among the best teams in the game at the time. I believe Notre Dame would have rivaled them, but otherwise, they dominated the scene.

Pappy's style was one of deep connection with his players. He had an unassuming, friendly and humorous manner that allowed people to truly enjoy his company and to relax around him. His players had tremendous respect and admiration for him. Pappy Waldorf was a symbol of all the greatness in college football. He produced some of the most exciting, best-drilled teams in the nation. He produced some of the great players, too.

I think Pappy would have been successful at any time, any place, at any level. He would have been a great professional coach. Of course, he was in charge of player personnel for the 49ers for a number of years, judging players and managing the draft, and he was highly respected in that area. He had a great football mind and was highly organized.

A lot of my own respect for Pappy and the work he did is related to my friendships with so many of his former players, along with the fact that I attended high school in the Bay Area and watched his games. During my years in high school, we would act as ushers at the Cal games, so Pappy was really big in my eyes. One particular year, 1948, when I was a youngster, I remember listening on the radio to Pappy's team beating USC. It was really a breakthrough for Cal, and it stopped the dominance of USC. From that point on, I was a fan of Pappy.

What made Pappy's teams so great was their precision execution - both on offense and defense - along with the intensity of their players and the fact that he always developed so much depth on his squads.

In terms of strategy, I don't think Pappy did anything that one would call revolutionary, other than the fact that his teaching techniques were tremendous - akin to Paul Brown and men like that. He brought that teaching and philosophy to the West Coast. That highly organized system of football was almost unique to Pappy. He was as solid and dependable and consistent as any teacher of football in the United States. It was the Pappy Waldorf system. If you saw his team, or a team of men who had played for him or coached under him, you knew right away that you were seeing Pappy Waldorf football.

It's no surprise that so many of his former players and coaches were successful teaching football themselves. John Ralston, who had such success in both college and pro football, is a good example of one of Pappy's players becoming a great coach himself.

In addition to being such a wonderful teacher and having teams that always were so fundamentally sound, Pappy had great depth on his teams. He had maybe 80 or 90 players on some teams during the post-World War II years at Cal. But it's one thing to have people around and another to use them properly. Pappy was quite willing to substitute his second and third units in games, putting them in as entire units, and they would play very well. You could hardly see any difference between his first unit and third unit. They were all so well-trained and committed to Cal football.

It's amazing to see how that commitment to Pappy went beyond the field and also long past these men's playing days. The very existence of Pappy's Boys - an organized group of

Pappy's former players - shows you what an impact he had on men 30, 40 or 50 years later. Many of them have become successful in their own careers, but they are still Pappy's Boys.

Pappy developed young men who went on to become prominent leaders in the nation. Others found success in the corporate and professional worlds. And they weren't just the stars or even starters for those Cal teams. Everyone on Pappy's squads made a commitment to excellence and learned so much from him. It has obviously had a notable effect later on in their lives.

That's just one more reason I believe Pappy Waldorf was truly a renaissance man who helped establish the greatness of football in America.

Big Game Night, November, 1978. (Left to Right) Roger Theder, Bill Walsh, Lloyd McGovern, Park Dingwell, Pappy Waldorf, Joe Ruetz and Dave Maggard.

INTRODUCTION

Every book has its own story.

I'm not referring to the subject, which in this case is the remarkable life and career of legendary football coach Pappy Waldorf, but to the story of the book itself.

Sometimes an author spends months or even years researching a pet project and then takes whatever time might be necessary to turn that work into a manuscript. Perhaps a literary agent or publisher calls with an idea, something marketable that the author can be commissioned to put into words.

I'm no stranger to these normal channels, having fought through the agonies and ecstacies of writing 11 books. But this one was different from the outset. So different, in fact, that the genesis of the book is a tale all its own.

Three people - one each from Texas, Arizona and Illinois - had a hand in this project, convincing me first, that the time for a book on Pappy Waldorf indeed had come and that I should drop whatever I might be doing to help create it.

Considering that I'm the managing editor of a daily newspaper and spend most days knee deep in administrative duties - plus writing a general interest column that appears on our front page five days a week; it's entirely accurate to say I wasn't exactly an easy sell.

At least not in the beginning.

The folks in question, however, were not easily dissuaded. Once the project was explained and I'd been drawn toward the fringes of Pappy's remarkable extended family, there was no turning back.

To understand how the saga unfolded, you need an introduction to Peter G. Brown, Roy Muehlberger and of course, my co-author John Greenburg.

I met Pete almost two decades ago, when he was running a landscaping business in Albuquerque. He'd grown up in Southern California, attended the University of New Mexico on a track scholarship and never lost his little-boy enthusiasm for sports. Over the years, in fact, Pete accumulated one of those gigantic memorabilia collections that eventually required a warehouse for storage.

During most of the 1990s, Pete and his wife Julia have been running a fascinating business called "History America Tours" from their base in Dallas. Essentially, the Browns set up specialty tours of Civil War battlefields, Indian war trails and almost any other history-oriented expedition you'd care to imagine. They hire an expert guide, while Pete handles the travel, accommodations and socializing along each route.

Being a gregarious sort, Pete generally develops friendships with most of his guests. "I really make an effort to connect with everyone sometime before a tour is over," Pete said, "which is why this one character really bothered me. We were near the end of a trip and I hadn't gotten into any sort of give-and-take with the fellow at all, so I took one last stab at it."

Pete discovered both he and his guest were from the Los Angeles area, which was a start. Then it turned out the gentleman had attended the University of California.

"I told him that was a coincidence," Pete said, "because I first started to fall in love with sports when my father took me down to watch the Cal football team practice for the 1950 Rose Bowl. I went on and on about it and mentioned that even all these years later, I could still recite every one of the Cal starters from that game. Well, I rattled off all these names and finally, the guy said, 'You missed one.'

"I asked who it was and he said, 'Me.' "

Despite that inauspicious start, Pete Brown got to know and ultimately become close friends with that one Bear starter he'd forgotten: Roy Muehlberger.

Pete and Roy since have become pals, confidants, the whole works. So one day in 1998, Pete phoned me and said, "There's somebody you've just got to meet."

It turned out that Pete had sent the Muehlbergers — Roy and Nancy — a copy of the biography I'd written on baseball star George Brett. Roy apparently enjoyed it and told Pete he had an idea for a great book that only lacked someone to write it.

This prompted a series of conversations among us.

I must have spent 50 hours on the phone with Roy before I ever laid eyes on the man. But Pete was right: Muehlberger was, indeed, one of the most fascinating individuals I'd run across - and that covers some serious territory.

Somewhere in all those discussions, I learned that Roy had seen a good share of the world while employed by Kaiser Industries, even surviving a bloody coup attempt against the government in Ghana. Then he and Nancy embarked on another career in the resort business. Currently, he is involved in an abalone farming venture. That's what you call diversified.

Roy was also a fanatical American history buff - not surprising when you consider how he met Pete Brown - and a man who runs with all his pursuits at breakneck speed. At that time, Roy's passion was to see a biography of Pappy Waldorf in every bookstore. In fact, he was adamant that a first-rate, professionally-produced book on Pappy would be a critical element in ensuring that the legacy of his former coach and hero would never fade away.

One of the curious aspects of Muehlberger's quest was that he had played only two years for Waldorf at California and the first of those seasons was spent with the Ramblers, a junior varsity team. Roy, though, has believed Pappy's influence on hundreds of people - himself included - had altered the course of their lives.

Muehlberger was an active member of a remarkable organization called Pappy's Boys, a group of Waldorf's former players, staff, friends and family that remains vibrantly alive nearly a half-century after any of them suited up for Waldorf at Cal.

Pappy's Boys, both the group and its individual members, have marked up plenty accomplishments over the years. They've funded scholarships, led a drive to commission the statue of Pappy that stands in Faculty Glade on the Berkeley campus and generally did everything in their power to carry on the Waldorf tradition of participation in society.

"It's not an accident that so many of Pappy's former players and coaches went on to other successes in their lives," Muehlberger said. "Look at these people and you'll be amazed at how many have made names for themselves."

I did and I was.

In fact, the men involved actually had done a book themselves in 1996, recounting the glorious seasons from 1948 through 1950, when Pappy's Cal teams stormed through three unbeaten regular seasons and made a trio of appearances in the Rose Bowl.

That book, which was coaxed into print by former Cal quarterback and Pappy's Boys major domo Dick Erickson, was a compilation of personal recollections. Many of Waldorf's former players and administrators wrote their memories of Pappy's influence on their lives after college. *Sports Illustrated* senior writer Ron Fimrite, also a Cal grad, edited the submissions and contributed an introduction.

"It was a headache putting it all together," Erickson said, "but once we'd heard from so many people, it was obvious the project was worthwhile. The downside was that our book was intended primarily for our own personal memories, for the group's enjoyment. As satisfying as it was, that book wasn't intended to sell to the general public.

"So we'd gotten our stories into print, and paid tribute to Pappy, but it was more like talking to each other than doing something to keep Pappy's fantastic legacy alive outside the group."

And that's what Muehlberger was determined to do when he contacted me.

Roy shipped me the Pappy's Boys book, along with a copy of Waldorf's book, *This Game of Football*. Eventually, Roy scoured his collection for such amazing items as a tape of an interview with Pappy recorded just weeks before his death in 1981, several videotapes of Cal games from the Waldorf era and perhaps even more important, a self-published book on the 1949 Rose Bowl written by Chicago-area football historian John Greenburg.

Ultimately, locating the Greenburg book was the pivotal moment in this quest to produce a mainstream-quality book about Pappy Waldorf.

You see, Greenburg initially researched football — specifically, college football in Big Ten country — as a permanent hobby. John was fascinated by Northwestern University, which was almost on his doorstep, but he also spent countless hours digging up newspaper clippings and interviewing people about the Notre Dame teams of the 1930s and 40s. Eventually, Greenburg became a walking encyclopedia of football trivia from that era and also became fascinated with the life and career of former Northwestern coach Pappy Waldorf.

In fact, following up on that stunningly researched book on the '49 Rose Bowl between Cal and Northwestern, John began concentrating on Pappy, full-time.

"I was overwhelmed by the character of the man, the way he taught, the positive influences he brought to everyone he met," Greenburg said. "And on the football, the more I got into the subject, the more I realized that Lynn Waldorf deserves to be recognized as one of the best and most influential coaches in college football history.

"I believe Pappy was one of the top five coaches of all time, and I don't say that lightly."

Greenburg was a natural collaborator for our book project. He started as a researcher, but contributed so much that ultimately, the only logical course was to sign him on as co-author. Many of the chapters in this book belong almost exclusively to John. I just tried to edit his material and occasionally just hop out of the way.

This wasn't exactly a bad choice, since by his own admission, John had compiled notes, quotes, tapes, clips, records, films and enough other background information that he'd studied Pappy Waldorf " ... from cradle to grave."

As it happened, I not only grew up in the San Francisco area, but had childhood ties to Waldorf from Pappy's post-Cal career with the 49ers. My dad and his partner in the accounting firm of Marshall & Cameron were retained as the 49ers' first official bookkeepers when the franchise was formed in 1946.

Thus we attacked the Pappy book from opposite directions: I went to California, while John delved into Waldorf's early days, and especially his 11-year tenure at Northwestern. Putting these far-flung pieces together was no picnic, so the cooperation and work-into-the-wee-hours help from everyone at Addax Publishing Group became critical to tying the project together.

Needless to say, all the wonderful men and women of Pappy's Boys, not to mention Pappy's daughters, Mary Louise and Carolyn, helped us every step of the way, even when the path seemed to be zig-zagging off in odd directions.

For all the books I've done and the satisfaction they've brought me, I have to say that the honor of participating in this project about this great man has been a genuine career highlight. As unusual as the inception and planning of this book might have been, not to mention the collective effort necessary to produce it, the result was worth every second.

I feel confident I can speak for John Greenburg and many others on one count — we hope Pappy would have been proud of this book.

- Steve Cameron
  Elk Ridge, Utah
  August, 1999

Chapter 1

FRESH MEMORIES

Imagine a beautiful spring night in the East Bay hills. The lights of San Francisco twinkle in the distance. A gang of rambunctious former college football players gather at the quarterback's house for an evening of good food and raucous conversation.

In truth, the event feels more like a season-ending banquet. Toasts are raised to good friends and great plays. Then the spotlight lands, as usual, on happy-go-lucky Frank Brunk, a scrappy halfback who backed up All-American Jackie Jensen in 1948 (Pappy Waldorf's first Rose Bowl team), then became part of Cal history in 1949.

The boisterous group recounts one defining electric moment, a stunning, almost miraculous kickoff return which clinched a must-win game. From a dozen perspectives, each man is almost shouting to add his thoughts. The group also rekindles an old beef — about a controversial call that perhaps sealed a heartbreaking bowl loss.

But mostly what you hear from this are kind words and hilarious stories about the beloved coach who brought them all — ex-jocks and now their wives as well — together for such a celebration. You almost expect the great man himself to stride across the patio and into the dining room, puffing his trademark cigar and calling for a cocktail in that booming bass voice. As surely as any football ever has been kicked or passed, the coach remains the life of this party.

As thrilling as the endless recitations of Brunk's kick return might be, however, no single play, victory or season begins to tell the story of Pappy Waldorf.

Pappy's legacy — as a man, husband, father, coach, teacher and role model — remains as huge as the fellow himself. This is noteworthy, indeed, since the one-time 210-pound tackle from Syracuse University later ballooned into the 300-pound range.

Now what any observer might find remarkable about this impromptu reunion of onetime players from the University of California, especially the freshness of their recollections, is that the youngest among them turned in his uniform more than 40 years ago. For most, it's been roughly a half-century.

But these are the Bears of Pappy Waldorf, men as devoted to their former coach a lifetime later as they were listening to his pre-game instructions in the late 1940s. What's almost eerie is that to everyone who knew Pappy, but especially to those who suited up for him, it all seems like just yesterday.

Pappy died in 1981, but in the spring of 1999, the gang around that dining room table were still Pappy's Boys. If 50 years had passed since they had played football together, they hardly seemed to notice.

Chapter 1

"It doesn't make sense, rationally," said Dick Erickson, who was hosting the party with his wife, Jan. "When you think of everyone's age, we should be in rocking chairs, barely able to remember what Pappy looked like. But he had such a marvelous effect on us, not just in college, but for the rest of our lives, that Pappy's presence seems like one long happy memory.

"I know lots of these guys and their families still think of Pappy's advice when they make important decisions. Not one of us hasn't thought, 'What would Pappy have done in this situation?' "

Even Pappy's daughters are amazed at the influence their father exerted on people near and far, over an incredible span of years.

"Sometimes I just can't believe these men and their wives can get together and their remembrances are so sharp and clear," said Mary Louise Osborne, the elder of Lynn and Louise Waldorf's two daughters. "Every time the group is together (at an annual reunion of the formal organization called Pappy's Boys), I have to remind myself that it's been 50 years.

"When you are with people my dad knew, everyone talks as if things just happened last week. I know that's a great tribute to him. The fact that he treated everyone as human beings - with humor and honesty - must have something to do with the way these memories just go on and on."

Mary Louise claims she will never quite get used to it, however. "Every time," she said, "I wonder how, after 50 years, these people can remember things so vividly."

So who was this gentleman whose influence seems to have made time stand still?

Well, Pappy Waldorf was a football man. But he was also so much more.

In a profession where the world often becomes totally one-dimensional, Waldorf truly embraced all life had to offer. He could appreciate a limerick as well as a Shakespearean play; he enjoyed bird watching, but also savored a good cigar, even mastering the unique skill of smoking a stogie in the shower. He was a man's man, a gentleman, a husband and a father. He was so respected and loved by his players and assistants, they nicknamed him Pappy.

Clark Kerr, the University of California's first chancellor, explained why the school approved placing a statue of Pappy in Faculty Glade when he wrote:

"He was an excellent teacher. He taught both football and character. He also was very supportive of academic requirements. He wanted to see his students continue through graduation.

"Thus, it is most appropriate that his life-size statue stands at the west end of Faculty Glade and that he is the only faculty member so recognized in that glade.

"During my time as chancellor at Berkeley, I considered him to be our best teacher; he had more moral impact on more students than did any other faculty member."

Pappy taught a course in football theory at Berkeley, which qualified him to be a member of the faculty, but he was a great teacher because he taught his students to have integrity. He stressed that their word was their bond and they should constantly strive to improve themselves. He taught the virtues of responsibility, patience and prudence. After graduation, his students went out into the world and taught these lessons to others.

Today's high-tech, project-oriented workplace would find Pappy's methods of organizing, training and motivating large groups as effective as they were during Cal's Rose Bowl Days.

Businesses faced with devising turnaround strategies could learn from one of football's supreme troubleshooters, a coach who turned five of the worst programs imaginable — three in the nation's toughest conferences — into instant winners.

Pappy's philosophy would fit well with our market-driven economy, for he was a consummate ambassador, a master at cultivating the media and communicating with people on their level.

Later in his football career, Pappy opened doors, not only for the San Francisco 49ers, but for the entire National Football League. Overall, Pappy's influence raised the status of professional football to national prominence.

America's youth have always sought heroes for inspiration, and Pappy was the walk-on who became an All-American, then the personification of a mentor - a man who devoted his life to helping youth help themselves.

Most appealing to the younger generation was that he made everything fun. People around him felt they were part of what he was doing, and all the while, he allowed them to be themselves.

Jim "Truck" Cullom, one of Waldorf's great Cal linemen, once said, "If I knew how Pappy did it, I'd bottle it."

To understand what made Pappy a coaching great, one must examine him in terms of the roles a college coach must play; namely: father, teacher, mentor and master organizer.

Pappy once was asked about his family and he replied, "We have two daughters, six grandchildren and two great-grandchildren. I have tried to be a good family man.

"Having the same tastes isn't the secret of a happy marriage. More important is tolerance, respecting your spouse as an individual and working together. Marriage is a partnership and mine has been a happy, rewarding one.

"Football was never a life-or-death matter with my wife or kids and I never pushed it. They were mild fans and that was fine with me. I think people have to live their own lives, do their own experimenting. It's like religion. You have your own beliefs, but you don't try to force them on other people.

"A child needs to feel parental support. I tell my daughters, 'Look, there's nothing you can possibly do that would ever alienate me from you. I trust you. I have faith in you. I want you to feel I will always be there for you. I'm not going to dictate. We want you to know you have the support of your mother and myself.'

"Oh, you can argue with your children, but I can't think of anything they could do that would turn me against my daughters. I could never kick a daughter out."

Being a father also requires spending as much quality time as possible with your family. When Pappy was hired at

Northwestern, the Waldorfs moved to nearby Wilmette and rented a house just a few blocks west of Dyche Stadium. Lynn turned it into a combination home and football headquarters.

Since the practice field and athletic department offices weren't far away, Waldorf saw his daughters off to school, met them for lunch, spent time with his family in the evening and still had time to prepare strategies for practices and games. He also made arrangements to meet with his assistants in his home without invading his wife's and two daughters' privacy. Pappy continued this form of "homework" when he moved to California.

Pappy also expressed fatherly qualities to his football players.

One day at a Cal practice, quarterback Paul Larson learned that even though Pappy thought the world of him, the coach wouldn't allow anyone to shirk his obligations to teammates or slack off in his leadership role.

Recalling the incident, Larson said, "I had made a speaking appearance at an Oakland Rotary Club luncheon, and when I returned to the campus for practice, there was a long line of players waiting to get taped. By the time I got out to the practice field, the team had already gone through their first two calisthenics.

"After the exercises, Pappy said, 'There are some guys here who don't think it's important to be on time for practice.' Then he told me and some second-stringers to take two punishment laps.

"As I ran, tears came to my eyes because it broke my heart to think that he thought so highly of me. It was like your dad who loves you, but doesn't tell you often enough. Later, I realized he did it to prove a point to the second-stringers. As one of the team's leaders, I always had to set a good example."

A dad is also a constant source of encouragement, as are coaches when freshmen make the huge leap to the varsity.

Don Piestrup was a Cal player confronted with this situation.

"I had two scholarship offers to go to college," he said. "One was to Cal for football, the other was to the Juilliard School of Music in New York. I figured that I could always take up music, but I'd only have one chance at football. So I went to Cal.

"There was just one problem - I was a 6-foot, 168-pound end. Before my sophomore year, I went to see Pappy and told him I didn't think I was big enough for PCC football.

"Pappy said, 'Piestrup, we need you.'

"I said, 'For what, the seventh team?'

" 'No,' he said, 'you'll be playing for us. Just make sure you keep getting second helpings at the training table. We need you to be over 180 pounds.' "

Don stuck with it and became a tough, 180-pound lineman on Cal's last Rose Bowl squad. He also went back to music, becoming a composer for Buddy Rich. He still writes musical scores for nationally televised commercials.

Pappy Waldorf proved to be a master communicator who was able to reach students on several different levels.

Chapter 1

Don Wilson was an African-American from Los Angeles who went to Cal on a football scholarship in the early 1950s. From the beginning of his college career, he wanted to get into sports management. In today's jargon, he would be called an agent.

"It wasn't a snap course," Wilson said. "There were over 30 books on (Waldorf's) reading list and the first day, he announced that everyone had to do a term paper.

"Pappy taught football's history as well as its theory. When he talked about Paul Robeson, I just knew I had to learn all about that man. You see, Paul Robeson had come to my elementary school and sang at an assembly. But no one said anything about him being a football player.

"In doing my research paper, I learned a great many things about Robeson, such as the fact that he graduated first in his law class. Paul Robeson was a true renaissance man and because of that term paper, he became a hero to me.

"When I was growing up, there were no real heroes on the West Coast. The only football games we could get on the radio were Notre Dame or the University of Pennsylvania. After Pappy arrived at Cal, though, Tidewater Oil started airing West Coast games on radio, and then television. Now, kids can listen to or see players they can identify with. Thanks to Pappy, kids finally have real sports heroes."

Learning from Waldorf motivated Wilson to earn a doctorate in history, and he went on to become dean and athletic administrator at Los Angeles City College. In a 10-year period, his school sent more young people to four-year colleges and universities on athletic or academic scholarships than any other junior college in the state.

Wilson also built a tremendous football program, touching the lives of many young men in the process. Two of his success stories are Rod Martin, a linebacker on two Super Bowl teams, and Vince Evans, who led USC to victory in the '77 Rose Bowl before playing almost two decades of pro ball.

Outstanding teachers are proud of their profession and seek to inspire youth to become part of it. So Pappy was always there to help aspiring coaches.

One example was Luther "Lukie" Phillips, a 5-foot-7, 160-pound scatback from Monterey who had been a very good high school player with excellent speed. Phillips, though, wasn't sure he was heavy enough or tall enough to play college football.

As he tells it, "I may have been fast, but I ran from fright."

This apprehension caused him a great deal of anxiety, because his ambition was to become a coach, but it was difficult to enter that field without first being a college athlete. Dan Dillon, Phillips' high school coach, saw that this uncertainty was affecting the young man, so Dillon had an idea.

Before moving to California, Dan had been an assistant football coach at Ohio State, and he had known Waldorf for several years. He took Lukie to Cal to see the coach folks called the "Wily Walrus."

"I'll never forget how gracious Pappy was," Phillips said. "After Coach Dillon and Pappy talked over old times, Pappy looked at me and in a low, gravelly voice, he said, 'If you were to look out over Memorial Stadium during football practice, you'd see tall men, short men, big men, thin men, men with all kinds of backgrounds. It takes many men, different in many ways to make a football team at the University of California. Welcome aboard, Lukie."

Phillips played for Cal's freshman team in 1948, then played for Zeb Chaney's junior varsity Ramblers the following year.

During Pappy's years at Berkeley, most of Cal's home dates were doubleheaders in which the Ramblers played a preliminary game to the varsity contest. The Rambler players would remain suited up for the day's main event and it was not unusual for a Rambler to play two games in one day, participating in both a junior varsity game and a lopsided varsity contest.

Because of this cross-participation, the Ramblers were treated equally with the stars of the varsity, with the same amenities each Friday night before a home game. The system obviously was tremendous for morale.

Cal's football record book does not list Lukie Phillips among Cal's all-time lettermen, but in reality, he played a lot of football. In fact, the Ramblers brought Cal a victory in a bowl game in 1949, when Phillips and his Rambler teammates defeated Humboldt State 40-26 in the Redwood Bowl.

Lukie scored five touchdowns in that game. All that was required for him to be successful was a chance to play.

As graduation neared, though, Phillips faced another dilemma - how to launch his coaching career. He found out then how far Pappy would go to help a young coach.

"I learned of an opening for a graduate assistant coach at San

Jose State, working for Bob Bronzan," Lukie said. "Coach Bronzan was a master at teaching the passing game and served as a consultant to Buck Shaw when Buck coached the Philadelphia Eagles. The job could launch me into a real coaching career, but graduate assistantships are generally reserved for graduates of that school.

"I told Pappy about this opening and next thing you know, he wrote a letter to Coach Bronzan and I got the job. I learned that a letter of recommendation from Pappy could get you just about any job on the West Coast."

That graduate assistantship led to a 41-year coaching career for Phillips, and he became the third-winningest coach in the history of California junior college football.

Pappy was an outstanding instructor who could teach almost anyone to be a good coach. The greatest example of this was Hart Fairclough, whose family moved to California just before he entered high school.

At 105 pounds, Hart was hardly big enough to play for his high school team, but football had gotten into his blood. He was born and raised in Evanston and had even attended some Northwestern games when Waldorf coached the Wildcats. Little did he know their paths would cross less than 10 years later.

Hart served in the Navy during World War II, then decided to go to college on the GI Bill and earn a teaching degree, because he still dreamed of becoming a football coach.

Eventually, Fairclough met with Frank Wickhorst, Pappy's predecessor at Cal. Wickhorst gave him permission to assist Cal's equipment manager, so Fairclough could attend all practices and home games, and thus, begin his study of football.

After Wickhorst was fired, Hart was worried that the new coach would not think highly of him hanging around on the periphery of the football team.

Fairclough met with Pappy and told him his story. Pappy was very supportive, saying, "Hey, Hart, I understand what you're trying to do. I think it's a great idea. I'll arrange for you to be part of the team. You can help with the equipment, but I especially want you to be at all the team meetings and take my course in football. I'll also see that you eat at the training table. If you're going to learn about football players, you've got to spend as much time as possible with them under all circumstances. Be sure to write down all the notes you can in a steno pad. This way, you'll be building your coaching manual."

Fairclough followed Pappy's suggestions, then worked as an assistant for John Ralston and Rod Franz at Mt. Diablo High in Concord, California. After paying his dues, Hart eventually became their head coach. During his 14-year career, his teams won five championships in six years.

Aided by the organizational skills and life lessons learned during their days of Cal football, many of Pappy's Boys emerged as champions in fields other than football. A few noteworthy examples:

• Tom Dutton, Vice-Chancellor of UC Davis;

• Dr. John Najarian, the first physician to transplant a kidney into a child;

- Jim Marinos, a prominent attorney in San Diego;

- Doug Duncan, the highest ranking member of the U.S. Secret Service on the West Coast;

- Ed Bartlett, who used the Waldorf principles of organization and motivation to build Golden Bear Ford into the Bay Area's second largest auto dealership;

- Chris Markey, a California Superior Court judge;

- Carl Van Heuit, who, as the head of the Traveler's Insurance Company's San Francisco region, applied Pappy's principles of management to win national sales contests;

- Bill Panttaja, the only member of Pappy's Boys fluent in Japanese, spent a lifetime furthering U.S.-Japan relations;

- Frank Brunk, president of the Northern California Golf Association;

- Nick Veliotes, who served as U.S. Assistant Secretary of State, then as Ambassador to Egypt under President Ronald Reagan.

Playing for Pappy clearly gave these men a head start on life by providing an environment which fostered fulfillment. Those who lived his lessons attest that anyone can become successful in any arena by following his methods.

The Waldorf years at Cal produced a setting in which good things could emerge, even from apparent tragedy.

On the opening day of the 1952 football season, Cal beat Pacific, 34-13, but that afternoon of victory ended sadly when Thelton Henderson, a Jefferson High recruit from L.A., suffered a broken leg on the last play of his first college game.

Henderson's injury ended his football career. As he lay in pain so great his eyes were forced shut, he heard a voice - the strong, yet soothing voice of a man consoling him. Henderson felt the man take his hand to reassure him.

When the pain subsided and he opened his eyes, Thelton saw a massive, gray-haired man. Although the man's face seemed very familiar, Thelton did not recognize him from Cal's athletic department.

Later, he learned that this gentle, compassionate individual was Earl Warren, the governor of California who was later appointed Chief Justice of the U.S. Supreme Court and orchestrated the unanimous court decision ending segregation.

Thelton Henderson lost a great deal that day - a college football career and possibly, a chance to play pro ball - but in the long run, he gained much more. On that painful afternoon, Thelton gained inspiration, a role model and a mentor in Earl Warren.

The leg healed, and Henderson eventually earned a legal education at the University of California. He went on to become the Chief Judge of the U.S. District Court of Northern California.

In the spring of 1952, Les Richter graduated from Cal as valedictorian of his class. During the following months, he learned that Pappy Waldorf would continue to provide him with sound advice.

"I was the first player selected in the NFL draft," Richter said, "when the league consisted of 12 teams. I was chosen by the

New York Yankees, but before I could start negotiating with them, the franchise was sold to 17 Texans in Dallas for $170,000. They were going to rename the team the Dallas Texans.

"Before I went to Texas to talk about a contract, I was briefed by Lynn O. Waldorf. He said, 'Son, if you have a desire to play professional football, that's fine and you'll be great, wherever you go. Just be sure they give you a full-time, 12-month salary so you can learn something that has a solid future.'

"After I arrived in Dallas, I talked to nine of the 17 owners and learned none had any interest in hiring me for the off-season. They offered to pay me $5,000 for the entire season. I owed some small debts to the university, so I asked for a $500 signing bonus, but they wouldn't agree. Since we couldn't come to terms, they put me on an airplane back to northern California. I told them before I left, they'd have to trade me to the San Francisco 49ers or the Los Angeles Rams.

"Soon after that, I got a phone call from Pete Rozelle, who was the publicity man for the Rams. He said, 'We'd like you to come to L.A. for a press conference announcing your signing with the Rams.' Then the Rams arranged a flight for me to L.A.

"When I arrived in Los Angeles, I met with Rozelle and Tex Schramm, the team's general manager, and the five owners - Dan Reeves, Ed Pauley, Fred Levy, Hal Seley and Bob Hope.

"I agreed to play for the Rams, then they said, 'Before we meet with the press, we've got to get this matter of a contract taken care of.' Pete Rozelle placed a light blue sheet of paper, which was a standard NFL player's contract, in front of me. I saw that it was for $7,500 per year, with a $500 signing bonus. I asked them, 'Where do I sign?'

"Then Pete Rozelle said, 'We'll also give you your shoes during your first year.' Pappy let me take the pads I had used at Cal. He did that for all of his players who went on to the pros. It was a way of preventing the discomfort or physical hazards involved in breaking in new equipment."

Richter went on to be a great performer for the Rams at linebacker, appearing in nine straight Pro Bowls. He accepted Ed Pauley's off-season job in commercial real estate development.

One of Pauley's projects was the construction and management of Riverside International Raceway. Les became the manager, then became more involved with automobile racing.

Today, Les Richter is one of the most powerful figures in motor sports, and recently opened California Speedway in Fontana.

Though his present occupation has nothing to do with football, Richter credits his success to his old college coach, Pappy Waldorf.

Pappy also served as a mentor for coaches - his assistants and other members of the profession.

"Pappy made it a point to be in contact with opposing coaches during the off season," said Paul Christopulos, the coach's right-hand man in the Cal athletic department. "One reason was to offer assistance or moral support to those whose jobs might be in jeopardy, a hazard of the profession that can affect anyone."

One of the coaches Pappy went to bat for was Marv Levy.

"When I was fired at Cal," Levy said, "I was disillusioned and ready to leave coaching to go into a more lucrative business. I lived five or six houses down from Pappy on Grizzly Peak. One day, he came to see me. He was tremendously supportive and told me, 'You're a good coach and you shouldn't leave the profession.' Then he asked if he could use the phone.

"He called the staff of William and Mary College, who were in the process of hiring a new coach. He told them, 'There's a man right here you should be interviewing.' Soon, I had an interview and I was hired.

"If it hadn't been for Pappy Waldorf, my coaching career would've ended over 30 years sooner."

Being highly organized is the most essential ingredient to becoming a successful coach. Waldorf's methods of organization were his greatest contribution to today's football theory. His manner of drawing up practice schedules, teaching fundamentals sequentially, analyzing game films and scouting opponents was emulated by Woody Hayes at Ohio State and copied by most of the coaches who either played for Hayes, worked for Hayes or observed his team. Eventually, the things Hayes learned from Waldorf became standard tools for football coaches everywhere.

Of all his traits that rubbed off on those around him, however, perhaps most remarkable was that Pappy was always himself — no pretenses, no phoniness. He was consistently low-key and could talk to anyone on that person's level.

Ultimately, Waldorf was great because he saw the game and his role in it realistically. He was the first to give credit, the last to take credit and never considered himself more important than

Chapter 1

his university.

Each day, Waldorf gave thanks for the privilege of being called "Coach" — and for having so many friends who called him "Pappy."

Chapter 2

MISSIONS IMPOSSIBLE

He was destined, almost certainly, to be a person of moral strength.

But a football coach?

Far less likely.

Lynn Waldorf was born October 3, 1902, in Clifton Springs, New York, the son of a well-respected Methodist minister named Ernest Waldorf.

The elder was the guidepost of young Lynn's life. Ernest had gone to Syracuse University, where he played on the baseball team and graduated in 1900. Recounting his life, Ernest Waldorf once said, "I started out intending to become a big businessman and succeeded to the extent that, as a young man, I was offered the managership of a large manufacturing concern. I experienced a change of purpose, however, and decided to enter the clergy."

While pursuing his ministerial studies, Ernest married the petite but feisty Flora Jannette Irish in 1902. They had a daughter and four sons.

Lynn's dad was ordained a Methodist minister in 1902, the same year he was married and Lynn was born. From 1902 through 1920, Ernest served at a number of pastorates in upstate New York and Buffalo. After earning a Doctor of Divinity degree, he became pastor of the First Methodist Church in Cleveland.

Reverend Waldorf was renowned for his sermons, which were inspirational speeches with such powerful messages and positive energy that churches were packed.

Yet the gifted preacher was an unpretentious man who didn't want a glass wall between himself and his flock, preferring to be called Ernie by church members.

"A true Christian gives his all to God, regardless," Ernest Waldorf preached, and because he lived those words, he won souls.

Every Sunday, the bishop would give five sermons at five churches. Flora played a vital role in this holy work, driving him to each place of worship in the family Buick. Their schedule was very tight, and once in a while, Flora was pulled over by the police for speeding. She would explain to the policeman, "Officer, I have to get the bishop to church in time to preach."

Flora often received a police escort instead of a ticket. She also spent a great deal of time on the telephone handling administrative details for her husband.

Lynn, the bishop's first son, developed a love of books as a young boy. The knowledge he gained was strengthened by the values and beliefs he learned from his father, kindling within him a devotion to honor, integrity, sportsmanship and fair play. He also learned to constantly search for new ideas, which inspired him to display initiative and express creativity throughout his life.

Lynn grew up in Cleveland, graduated from East High and went to Syracuse University because his father's status in the clergy afforded him the luxury of a partial scholarship. The youngster worked odd jobs to pay the remainder of his expenses, looking for rugged work during the summer to build his strength.

Considered too short to make the freshman squad at Syracuse, Lynn played the next three years for Chick Meehan's varsity and twice was named to Walter Camp's All America team. Syracuse's record was 24-4-3 during that time.

Lynn also rowed for the Syracuse crew, which was unusual due to his 210-pound size. The future coach later explained his rowing days by saying that the physically demanding sport could toughen up just about anyone.

The most rewarding experience of Waldorf's college days, though, was winning the hand of Louise McKay, a very refined young lady with a remarkable range of interests that included basketball, modern dance and bird watching.

Lynn and Louise were married August 14, 1925, in LaGrange, Illinois.

Nearly three-quarters of a century later, everyone who knew the couple insists they were a team in every sense of the word.

Later in life, for instance, Lynn became interested in bird-watching, as well, which led him to champion environmental causes long before it was popular.

Conversely, as the wife of a man who would devote his professional career to football, Louise also learned to function as his assistant.

John Ralston, who played two years for Waldorf at Cal and later became a successful college and NFL coach, has frequently said he and his wife patterned their lives after the Waldorfs.

"Louise was so important," Ralston said. "She entertained, hosted events and made friends with the wives and girlfriends of players so they would feel included. She was amazing and I've never forgotten it.

"Pappy and Louise were the ultimate role models for how a coach and his wife should be. My wife, Patty, and I tried to emulate them. If we succeeded even partly, I'm very proud."

One of the more interesting yarns involving Lynn Waldorf's college days at Syracuse is surrounded by an aura of mystery: Did Lynn actually stand up his bride-to-be, Louise McKay, for a school dance because of distress over losing a football game?

Perhaps no one can answer this with certainty, but the puzzle has made for good storytelling through the years.

Here's the account from Chick Meehan, Waldorf's coach at the time Syracuse lost to arch-rival Colgate in 1923:

"We lost 16-7, our only loss that year, but there wasn't an observer in the press box who didn't concede that the best player on the field was Lynn.

"There was a dance that night at the Tri Delta house. Lynn was supposed to escort the coed who is now Mrs. Waldorf, but he didn't show up. Finally a freshman came over from the Pi Kappa Alpha house and told his worried fiancee, 'Mr. Waldorf won't be over tonight.'

"I found him in the basement of his fraternity house, still reviewing the day's misfortunes and muttering to himself. 'Listen Lynn,' I said, 'we lost that ball game, but not because of you. You were the best lineman on the field today, so what are you worrying about?'

" 'What does that matter, coach, we finished second, didn't we?' Waldorf answered from the depths of the coal pile. 'You told us how to win and we didn't do it. It was our fault.' "

Now, that exchange - indeed, Lynn's non-appearance for a date — may or may not have happened. At least not that way.

Carolyn Waldorf Pickering, the younger of Pappy's two daughters, doubts that her dad ever left his future wife standing alone.

"I suppose it's possible," Carolyn said, "I've heard that story just like everybody else has. But neither my mother nor father ever mentioned it to us. I'm almost positive they would have, because the whole thing seems so out of character for Dad.

"It just wasn't his nature to ignore a responsibility, whether it was a date or a meeting or anything else. Since no one in the family ever mentioned it, I doubt that it really took place."

One aspect of the story, however, rings true. Somewhere along the way - possibly after that infamous loss to Colgate - Louise gave Lynn a piece of advice which ultimately became a critical component of his coaching philosophy.

"Football is a game," Louise told him. "And if you can't have fun, it's too bad."

Waldorf not only took those words to heart, he quoted them often to his players and repeated the phrase in his book, *This Game Of Football.*

Whether Lynn stood up his beloved Louise so he could brood in despair remains very much in question. But there is no doubt his future bride helped shape Lynn's view of football.

What's harder to explain is just how Lynn Waldorf came to be a lifelong football coach.

"Sheer happenstance," Lynn called it.

It's easy to follow the trail of victories and friends the Waldorfs spread across the country over the years, but it certainly wasn't preordained when the young couple set out to make a life for themselves in 1925.

For one thing, Lynn majored in sociology and psychology, hardly the academic background you'd expect for a future coach.

Nevertheless, Lynn's prowess on the field, along with his father's widespread influence, gave him the entree into the coaching world. However, he didn't realize at the time what the job entailed.

Waldorf was offered a high school coaching job in Erie, Pennsylvania, but turned it down because he didn't think he would feel comfortable teaching at that level.

Chapter 2

Meanwhile, Bishop Ernest Waldorf contacted Dr. Eugene Antrim, president of Oklahoma City University, an 800-enrollment Methodist institution.

Ernest no doubt hoped for an opening in the sociology department, but Dr. Antrim startled Lynn by offering him $4,000 a year — no pittance at the time — to coach football, basketball and track, in addition to teaching and filling the position of athletic director.

"I didn't know what I was getting into," Waldorf admitted. "I coached because I had to."

If ever a man was fit for the calling, however, it was Lynn Waldorf.

The Oklahoma City University Goldbugs were coming off a disastrous 1-7 season, and for as long as they had been a member of the Oklahoma Collegiate Conference, they hadn't won a single league contest. The school had never held a homecoming, let alone played a homecoming game. The young coach wondered if he made the right choice when he saw Goldbug Field's 1,200 seats — especially compared to Academy High's 15,000-seat facility back in Erie.

Lynn had never studied coaching, but his love of reading and his desire to absorb new ideas provided him with a solid background in the principles of leadership. He was fascinated by the Civil War and throughout most of his life, sought out every book written on the subject. He was enthralled by how young men of warm affection, susceptible to the tenderest emotions, could fight relentlessly during our nation's bitterest conflict.

Waldorf began comparing football coaches to military generals and through that process, he arrived at conclusions which prepared him to coach.

Through his reading, the young coach learned that the best generals were those who led by example. He also discovered that exemplary leaders gained their men's loyalty by sharing their experiences and giving the enlisted men a chance to prove themselves.

Lynn knew he had a degree of credibility based on his reputation as a player, but he had to prove his football savvy to young men he had never met.

He also had to be prepared, not only for games but for practices, so his players would trust his judgment.

Lynn believed it was crucial to hold highly-organized practices. Otherwise, his players wouldn't take the games seriously, which is the undoing of any team. He also learned the true enemy of men in combat is boredom.

The young coach decided that everyone on the team must constantly be involved in the action, otherwise there would be no fun in what was supposed to be sport.

Waldorf read of generals who failed because they committed acts of desperation after they grew impatient, and couldn't handle frustration. He came to the conclusion that patience is essential to coaching.

Since he was starting from scratch, Waldorf considered the fundamentals of blocking, tackling and getting off the line of scrimmage with the snap of the ball to be the most important arts to be mastered.

He reasoned that if players performed these fundamentals well, they could be victorious within any offensive or defensive system. This focus on fundamentals remained the basis of Waldorf's philosophy for his entire coaching career.

Only 14 players turned out for the first practice Waldorf conducted at Oklahoma City, so he persuaded additional students to suit up. The starting 11 for his first OCU team included six players without high school football experience.

The line averaged only 158 pounds, so the backfield actually was bigger than the line, averaging 163 pounds. Worst of all, these players' lack of size was exceeded only by their lack of footspeed.

This wasn't exactly a bunch of ragamuffins, though. They had talent and loads of grit. Best of all in the new coach's mind, they were good kids — honest and eager to learn.

Mastering plays and striving for precise execution as a unit enabled Waldorf's players to trust themselves and each other. They also learned the importance of playing smart football.

Waldorf told them: "Whether you're on offense or defense, always be aware of down and distance. If you know that and concentrate on when the ball is snapped, you won't jump offsides."

Lynn also taught his new team blocking fundamentals, and through repetitive drills, the Goldbugs began to block with precision. Once they mastered blocking, they began playing solid defense. The technique of blocking is nearly the same as that of tackling, the only difference being that the rules allow defenders to use their hands.

"Just remember," Waldorf cautioned his players, "to keep your eyes on the ball carrier's belt buckle."

Waldorf coached his first game on September 25, 1925, in Tahlequah, Oklahoma, against Northeastern Oklahoma Teachers College. His lightweight, inexperienced, slow-footed squad lost 3-0, but as Lynn said later, "At least we had the satisfaction of keeping 'em out of the end zone."

Lynn didn't take that loss as a personal defeat and didn't want his players to feel that way, either.

The Goldbugs played another road game the following Friday, this time in Claremore against Oklahoma Military Academy. The offense had not yet jelled, and Bill Moore's three field goals accounted for all the Goldbugs scoring, but it was a momentous day for Waldorf, as he bagged his first coaching victory, 9-6.

Oklahoma City's success didn't carry over into the following week, though, as the Bugs lost their first home contest of the 1925 season to Southwestern Oklahoma, 6-0.

On October 17, OCU edged Phillips University at home, 3-0, for the first conference victory in school history — despite being outweighed on the line 42 pounds per man.

The Goldbugs' success bordered on the miraculous, because after the first four games, Bill Moore's toe had produced all his team's points. Moore, it would turn out, was more than just the coach's one reliable threat in the early days. By the next season, Moore had also become Waldorf's best recruiter.

Oklahoma City's final 1925 record was 4-6, but it had been the school's most successful season. Waldorf achieved another minor miracle by fielding a team fans would actually pay to see. That season's gate receipts totalled a best-ever $87.40.

Waldorf was also the school's track coach, but since he had no facility in which to hold meets, he came up with a creative solution.

Years later, Pappy loved to tell the tale of how he solved the problem.

"Part of the campus was 16 acres of unused cotton field with a ravine running through it," he said. "That made a naturally banked horseshoe curve. The school's president agreed that it could be transformed into a running track, but unfortunately, there was no money for the project.

"I decided to make it a community project. I asked the head of the mathematics department to figure the curves. One player's uncle was in the state legislature and agreed to have the state highway department leave a road grader at the campus and forget about it for a week. A sergeant in the Army Reserve unit hooked the grader up to his tractor, and since I chipped in for the gasoline, he pulled the grader along the straightaways and swung it around the curves.

"Then I contacted the manual training department of a local high school and they agreed to make hurdles if I supplied the wood."

That was how Waldorf managed to construct an athletic facility for the sum of $6.94 — dirt cheap, even by 1925 standards.

George B. Goff, Oklahoma City's fire chief, told local writers he was impressed with Waldorf's treatment of his players, as well as his contributions to the community. Goff said, "He was the first to put some of his boys on the fire department. I guess I attended a hundred of his practices and I never heard him raise his voice.

"Lynn would take some kid who had never played football and would have him tearing his toes off for him in two weeks. He never got tough, no matter how dumb the boy was."

On the family front, 1926 was a momentous year. Louise and Lynn celebrated the birth of their daughter, Mary Louise.

Then during that summer, Bill Moore mentioned to Waldorf, "Coach, there are a couple of guys in my hometown, Carnegie, Oklahoma, who could play here."

The player's suggestion started a procession of Carnegie athletes to the Oklahoma City campus, players who would contribute to the team's success. Waldorf, however, never once set foot in that Oklahoma town.

One of Moore's Carnegie recruits was Bob Eaton, a lanky end and outstanding athlete who not only excelled in football, but also set a conference record in the high hurdles.

The first time Waldorf saw Eaton punt, he noticed that Bob held the ball and kicked in an unorthodox manner. When that punt sailed 50 yards, though, Lynn decided he wouldn't try to change Eaton's kicking motion.

Waldorf did, however, want Eaton to learn to emphasize accuracy. Bob wasn't happy at first and voiced his displeasure when he said, "Hell, coach, that'll never work."

Waldorf insisted on doing it his way, stressing it would be best for the team if Eaton learned the tactic. Bob followed Lynn's instructions because he was determined to prove the coach wrong, but then displayed accurate placement punting during several winning seasons.

Eaton was exhilarated and took great pride not only in his own success, but in having a coach who knew football. From this experience, Waldorf learned you can't control people's motives, and sometimes individuals will follow instructions for their own reasons.

In addition to being an outstanding coach, Waldorf proved to be an exceptional administrator and promoter. He oversaw the financing and construction of a $150,000 gymnasium, complete with two swimming pools — one for men and one for women.

The young athletic director also established a working relationship with nearby Classen High School. The Comets agreed to play their home games at Goldbug Field on Saturdays.

Lynn also marshaled support for increasing Goldbug Field's seating capacity to 7,500 and adding lights to the facility for night games. It made good business sense to play home games with Friday-evening kickoffs rather than compete with University of Oklahoma games on Saturday afternoon.

Oklahoma City went 5-4-1 in 1926, and then in 1927, aided by Fire Chief Goff's employment of OCU players as part-time firefighters, Waldorf was able to attract a couple of talented recruits — Leroy "Ace" Gutowsky and Basil Wilkerson, a Native American.

The Goldbugs played an ambitious schedule that included the

Haskell Institute from Lawrence, Kansas, a powerhouse that hadn't lost a game in two years. The demand for tickets to the Haskell game was so great, the contest was moved to Western League Park, home of the city's minor league baseball team.

It was the first time Oklahoma City played before a crowd of more than 10,000, and OCU escaped with a spectacular 7-0 victory, breaking the Indians' 26-game unbeaten streak.

Oklahoma City's final 1927 record was 8-1-2. Due to a 0-0 tie with Oklahoma Baptist, the Bugs had to settle for a share of the Oklahoma Collegiate Conference title. Only a 7-0 road loss to Tulsa kept them from laying claim to being the best team in the state.

By this time, Oklahoma City's football team had acquired tremendous talent. Five of Waldorf's players went on to perform in the National Football League, including Gutowsky, who starred at fullback for the 1935 champion Detroit Lions.

Waldorf enjoyed immediate success at Oklahoma City — winning a conference championship, filling and enlarging the stadium, overseeing construction of a classy new gymnasium and getting a makeshift track built for practically nothing.

"I really believe the combination of character and talent for organization, along with dealing with people, would have made Dad successful at anything," Waldorf's daughter Mary Louise said many years later.

"When Carolyn and I and the rest of family look back, we can see why Dad was a great coach. He could have been great in any job."

Following three years of transforming the football team from a joke to a point of university pride at Oklahoma City, Waldorf left to take the only assistant's position he ever would hold, signing on as freshman coach at the University of Kansas.

Lynn's objectives involved career advancement, learning more about the coaching profession and refining what he had already put into practice.

Accepting the position at KU ultimately was a great move. Waldorf not only added 17 hours of graduate work in anthropology to his educational credentials, he also met the legendary Amos Alonzo Stagg.

Stagg, who is considered the greatest coach in collegiate history, told Waldorf that the key to his profession was his relationship with his players.

"I loved all my players," Stagg said. "Some I had no respect for and some I disliked, but I loved them all the same."

Stagg also told young Lynn that he wouldn't be able to judge the success of his teams until 20 years after the fact, when he could see how they had fared in life.

Another of Stagg's commandments stuck with Waldorf, and he carried it like a torch throughout his life: "Your players are your pupils, with more interest in your subject than any of their other classes. For that reason, you should be the best teacher in the school."

In 1929, Waldorf was lured away to Oklahoma A&M College in Stillwater, a school which had just committed to big-time football by joining the Missouri Valley Conference.

Again, it was a case of long odds and slim resources.

Again, Waldorf had the answers.

This time, his secret was manipulating numbers, a theme that would reappear down the road. Waldorf organized a huge freshman team into three squads, using one as a scout team while scheduling as many freshman games as possible.

The Aggie frosh didn't win a game that first year, but Pappy saw that morale was rising and kids were committing themselves to the program.

The varsity went 4-3-2 in 1929, but more importantly, the Ags defeated in-state rivals Tulsa and Oklahoma City, and tied Oklahoma.

The following year, the Aggies made a two-game road trip into Big Ten Country that put Oklahoma A&M on the nation's gridiron map.

The first stop on the junket was Iowa City, for a game against coach Burt Ingwersen's Iowa Hawkeyes. Six minutes from the end of a scoreless game, Waldorf decided to shake up the Hawks by sending in his "Pony Backfield," none of whom weighed over 150 pounds. They were a lightweight but fast unit that ran pass plays from a Double Wing formation, sending four receivers downfield.

In the last four minutes of that game, Clarence Highfill completed two of three throws for 31 yards and a touchdown. Oklahoma A&M's 6-0 lead held up for the school's first-ever win over a Big Ten opponent.

After a week in Terre Haute, Indiana, preparing for a game against Indiana University, Waldorf's Cowboys battled the Hoosiers to a 7-7 tie.

Chapter 2

In addition to bringing home a win and a tie, the team deposited their share of the gate receipts, $15,000, into the A&M athletic department's bank account - a major windfall during the Oklahoma Dust Bowl days.

The team's record that year was 7-2-1, and the Cowboys were champions of the Missouri Valley Conference.

Waldorf's salary increased to $5,700 in 1931, when he assumed the duties of athletic director. He also faced the difficult task of selling tickets to football games during the Great Depression, when money was extremely tight.

Concrete stands had been added to Lewis Field, which increased the seating capacity to 13,000. Lynn was forced to think of creative ways to fill the expanded stadium, to keep those new seats from getting dusty.

In a unique move, Waldorf scheduled most of Oklahoma A&M's home games for Friday nights, the tactic he had used successfully at Oklahoma City. Lynn wanted to avoid competition from Saturday contests hosted by Tulsa and OU.

Waldorf meticulously planned each Friday evening of the football season to ensure that additional festivities surrounded each game, with added inducements like barbecues or steak fries. In addition to the usual bands and cheerleaders, cowboys mounted on horseback in full western-show regalia delighted the crowd by performing rope tricks and stunts on horseback.

When Haskell Institute played in Stillwater, more than 5,000 members of neighboring Native American tribes used the occasion to hold a pow-wow. Local Pawnees added to the pageantry by performing their ceremonial dances at halftime.

Waldorf also staged a "Night Carnival" on September 25, 1931, during which he divided the 56 players on his squad into two teams and gave the fans two complete football games for the price of one — in addition to a night filled with music, food, fun and fireworks.

Oklahoma A&M won both games, defeating Bethany College of Kansas, 32-0, and Northeastern Oklahoma, 25-0.

A&M's overall record in 1931 was 8-2-1, with the Cowboys' only losses coming at the hands of Big Ten power Minnesota and Waldorf's old friends from Oklahoma City University.

In 1932, Lynn's pay was reduced to $4,500 because of the negative impact of the Great Depression on the region. Even though Lynn and Louise faced added expenses when their second daughter, Carolyn, was born that year, the financial setback didn't diminish his joy or enthusiasm in the least.

Cowboy fans were bullish about the team's prospects that year, and with good reason. A&M ran up a 9-0-2 mark against accredited four-year college opponents — the only such season in the school's history.

Waldorf's 'Pokes opened their 1933 season with a tough 6-0 home loss to the University of Colorado. Then they lost a 19-13 decision to Oklahoma City at Goldbug Field.

OCU's coach was Wes Fry, a former Classen High coach who, by that time, had become a close friend of Waldorf's.

The Cowboys' schedule didn't get any easier. Eight days later, Oklahoma A&M squared off with powerhouse Southern Methodist at Dallas' Fair Park Stadium, which later became the Cotton Bowl, and brought home a 7-7 tie.

SMU viewed the stalemate as a setback for a team touted as the Southwest Conference champions, while the Aggies entered the contest with a record of 1-2.

That tie actually got Oklahoma A&M rolling again. The Cowboys won five games in a row to clinch a second consecutive Missouri Valley title.

The season ended with a 13-0 Thanksgiving Day win over traditional rival Oklahoma, making A&M's final record 6-2-1.

Waldorf's magic was back. His Oklahoma A&M teams went 34-9-7 over five seasons and won four Missouri Valley Conference championships. He still holds the Cowboys' highest coaching winning percentage (.735).

"The thing I was proudest of," Waldorf said later, "was that from the beginning of the second quarter in that first year, we had 19 scoreless quarters against the University of Oklahoma."

Another change was taking shape in Waldorf's coaching persona. He had already learned about relationships with players, mastered the art of dealing with alums, boosters and the media — and he had discovered how numbers, or depth of players at each position, could help almost any college football program.

So Waldorf turned back to fundamentals: blocking, tackling, firing off the line of scrimmage quickly.

"Teaching fundamentals properly is the best test of a coach's teaching ability," Waldorf said. "Working on fundamentals through repetitive drills tends to be monotonous, so every coach must be creative in organizing practices to keep the players' enthusiasm up.

"Also, players hit plateaus - they get to a point where, try as they might, they just can't seem to get any better and they become discouraged. When this happens, the coach must encourage the player.

"Teaching fundamentals properly means that the coach must first explain the technique. Then, the technique must be demonstrated properly. Next, the players go through it in slow motion. After that, it is repeated over and over until it is done just right. Finally, we polish it until it becomes a real gem."

This philosophy of working on fundamentals until they become second nature became Lynn Waldorf's coaching signature.

In the decades he spent at Northwestern (1935-46) and then at California (1947-56), Pappy's teams invariably were fundamentally sound.

They hit. They tackled. They burst off the line on time — so fast, in fact, that many opposing teams complained that Pappy taught his players to anticipate the snap count and explode a split-second early.

Waldorf's theory, which has been proven repeatedly at every level of football, is that a fundamentally sound team will almost always be competitive. When you add a reservoir of talent to that fundamental discipline, and complement it with depth, well...

That's when you dominate.

Shortly after the end of the 1933 season, Alvin "Bo" McMillin left Kansas State to become head coach at Indiana, and recommended to K-State's athletic board that Waldorf replace him in Manhattan.

Kansas State offered Lynn the job, which included a pay raise to $5,000 per year. The new position allowed him to coach at a school with a bigger football budget, which scheduled intersectional contests and which competed in the more prestigious Big Six Conference.

Waldorf arrived in Manhattan on March 28, 1934, with no idea of the welcome he was to receive. Three bands headed a parade from the campus to the center of town and a crowd of 2,000, though shivering in a chilly wind, cheered and sang at the top of their lungs for 45 minutes.

The rally was broadcast throughout the state. When sports writers asked Waldorf how he thought the team would do, they found the new coach with a voice like rolling thunder to be overly cautious. The exact quote: "Reserve last place for Waldorf."

Later, people learned that pessimistic predictions were just part of Lynn's style.

Waldorf was thrilled to hire his good friend Wes Fry, the coach from Classen High and Oklahoma City University, as his chief assistant. Fry had been an All-American halfback at the University of Iowa, played in the first East-West Shrine Game in 1926 and then became a teammate of Red Grange with the New York Yankees of the American Football League.

While playing in the pros, Fry earned his law degree from Iowa, and decided to settle down with his wife, Fran, in Oklahoma City. Soon enough, however, he was asked to coach at Classen, and like Lynn, he began a lifetime of coaching out of "sheer happenstance."

Waldorf needed all the help he could get in a situation that easily could have blown up in his face. Since the Big Six Conference didn't sanction freshman football games, Lynn inherited 10 frosh who had been neglected and used as cannon fodder in scrimmages with the varsity.

One of those sophomores-to-be was Caesar Augustus Cardarelli, a 5-foot-7, 200-pound lineman from Republic, Pennsylvania. A handsome young man, he was nicknamed "Duck" because he had a habit of waving his arms as he spoke. Cardarelli's body was as hard as anthracite, though, and he impressed his pals by shattering baseball bats over his biceps.

Lynn inherited a rugged situation, since the team's success in 1935 would almost surely hingle on the play of those 10 sophomores who hadn't been given a chance to develop into regulars.

Worse still, upperclassmen Oren Stoner and Lee Shaffer had played barely enough in 1933 to earn their letters.

Matters were complicated by a lack of dedication on the part of a few veteran players. Waldorf had been stranded in Manhattan with a collection of prodigal sons.

"We won our first game against Fort Hays State," Waldorf said. "Then I took a 26-man squad on a two-week East Coast road trip by rail, and for practically all those Kansas kids, it was the first time they'd been outside the state."

The Wildcats' first opponent on the junket was Manhattan College, coached by Waldorf's college mentor, Chick Meehan, in Ebbets Field, home of the Brooklyn Dodgers.

Unfortunately, rain began falling the previous day and

continued through the first half of the game, turning the field into a sea of mud.

Ralph Churchill blocked a punt late in the first quarter, giving Kansas State the ball on Manhattan's 3-yard line. Two plays later, Ted Warren scored and K-State led, 7-0.

Manhattan rallied, though, blocking one of Stoner's punts early in the second quarter. The loose ball rolled out of bounds at K-State's 2-yard line, setting up a one-play touchdown drive to tie the score at 7-7.

Still in the second quarter, Kansas State fumbled the ball at midfield. Manhattan launched a scoring drive that resulted in a 13-7 edge at halftime.

In the third quarter, Stoner's 20-yard run sparked a march that finished with his 5-yard toss to Churchill for a game-tying touchdown.

Late in the 13-13 ballgame, K-State blocked another punt and eventually reached Manhattan's 3-yard line. With time running out, Stoner missed a game-winning field goal attempt in that quagmire from an impossible angle.

The Wildcats had ridden thousands of rail miles, all for a 13-13 tie, but they had impressed the New York sports writers with their will to come from behind.

A week later, Marquette appeared ready to blow out K-State as sophomore halfback Ray Buivid carried 28 times for 207 yards and two touchdowns. The Hilltoppers built an apparently insurmountable 27-0 lead with 10 minutes remaining in the third quarter.

But Army Armstrong sprinted for two scores and Stoner connected with Red Elder for a sensational 51-yard touchdown. The game went into the books as a 27-20 loss for Kansas State, but it was a breakthrough for Waldorf's young team.

After surviving that heartbreaking road trip, Lynn's troops believed they could handle any team, any time, any place.

When K-State faced Oklahoma, game day in Norman came up overcast with gusty winds. Waldorf felt his team was in for it because OU had Cash Gentry, a rare combination of All-American tackle and exceptional punter. Gentry had also perfected a technique of punting effectively against a fierce wind.

The Sooners couldn't have asked for more under the prevailing weather conditions.

In the second quarter, Oklahoma scored to take a 7-0 lead. Then just before the end of the first half, K-State marched to the OU 6, but ran out of downs.

Oklahoma couldn't gain yardage, though, so Gentry was forced to punt from his end zone. Dean Griffing anticipated the snap count and gave the Sooners' center a right cross with his forearm. Then he lifted the lineman, gave him a legal head-slap along the earhole and broke through the line.

All that scuffling reduced the snap to a loose football skidding on the turf. When Gentry attempted to pick it up, Griffing flattened him in the end zone for a safety.

Instead of being shut out at halftime, the Wildcats were less than a touchdown away, trailing 7-2. Griffing's play proved to be the winning margin in Kansas State's 8-7 victory.

After that survival act, the Cats began to cruise through the conference schedule.

Then came a showdown with the Nebraska Cornhuskers. Coached by football legend Dana X. Bible, they were an imposing group. A sellout crowd of 22,000 gathered in Lincoln on a sunny but cold Thanksgiving Day to see the game that would decide the Big Six Championship.

Two K-State interceptions harnessed the Huskers, and although Nebraska played most of the first half in the Wildcats' end of the field, the Cornhuskers were ahead by only a touchdown at intermission.

In the K-State dressing room, the normally cool-tempered Waldorf was noticeably angry because George Maddox was playing back on his heels, getting shoved around by a much smaller man.

Waldorf asked the player, "Maddox, how much do you weigh?"

Maddox replied: "230."

"So tell me," Waldorf said, "how can a 185-pound end push you all over the place? You're not playing like you mean it. What does it take to get through to you? You'll be the sorriest man in the world if your teammates lose because of what you didn't do."

There was no reaction from Maddox, just a blank stare. And then the coach who never before raised his voice turned away from Maddox and he shouted, "Aw, get the hell outta here!"

Waldorf's display of anger scared his players. They saw a side of their coach they never wanted to see again. Lynn's sudden transformation catapulted them out of the locker room and onto the field.

Waldorf remembered the day this way: "Two games in one. Nebraska went up and down the field all afternoon, and how they scored only seven points, I'll never know.

"Then, with seven minutes left in the third quarter, it was as if you drew a curtain, then the next act and a new game began."

The Cornhuskers managed only one more long drive in the third quarter, and it was stopped at the Wildcat 20. Then the K-State offense exploded for three touchdowns and a convincing 19-7 triumph that earned them their only conference championship in school history.

Two thousand jubilant Kansans who had made the trip to Lincoln tore down Nebraska's goal posts and Kansas Governor Alf Landon wired his congratulations.

Northwestern University's athletic director Kenneth "Tug" Wilson also made the trek out to witness the K-State victory. But Wilson was actually on a recruiting mission. He had already decided he wanted Waldorf as his coach.

Chapter 3

PURPLE HEAVEN

This truly was the big time.

Northwestern competed in a more prestigious league than Kansas State. Ticket prices in the Big Ten Conference were twice that of the Big Six, crowds packed huge stadiums week after week, and the press and public agreed that the best football was played there.

However, NU did not have the football tradition enjoyed by the conference's other schools. Northwestern was the last school in the Big Ten to hire a full-time football coach, so Midwestern sports writers never considered Northwestern a serious contender for the Big Ten Championship.

The arrival of Tug Wilson as NU's athletic director in 1925, though, was the impetus for a major transformation at the campus along Chicago's North Shore.

In 1927, 32-year old Dick Hanley was hired to coach the

Wildcats. Hanley was one of the youngest coaches in the Midwest at that time, and the first man from the West Coast to become a Big Ten coach.

At first, he was just what Northwestern needed. Hanley was a tough guy coaching a tough game. However, Hanley lacked style, he was outspoken at the wrong times and he refused to play politics.

This eventually proved to be his undoing at the Methodist university in Evanston.

Hanley was a devout Catholic who attended mass five days a week. Early in Hanley's career at Northwestern, he received a subtle message that he should maintain a low profile while practicing his faith.

NU was also known for its stiff entrance requirements, and to many of its faculty members, a Phi Beta Kappa from Washington State didn't count for much. Dick Hanley was a true man of the west, and as time passed, he realized he did not fit in at NU.

Dick Hanley's reign hit bottom in 1933, when Northwestern's record was 1-5-2. That team displayed unique ineptitude, scoring a total of 25 points, all of which came in a game against Indiana.

Hanley had his fans, though, including members of the Northwestern Club of Chicago, local military veterans groups and Evanston "townies" who felt Tug Wilson was preoccupied with kowtowing to power brokers like city father Charles Gates Dawes.

Hanley's devotees became embarrassingly vocal about the

treatment their favorite Irish-Catholic coach was receiving from the Methodist university, and a split appeared within the campus community.

Among those displeased with Hanley's divisive effect on the university was Bishop Ernest Waldorf, who at that time was a member of Northwestern's board of trustees. He had a solution for the "Hanley Problem," but he had to present his idea to the right person at the right time.

The occasion presented itself at a luncheon held by the Women's Christian Temperance Union, with coach Amos Alonzo Stagg as guest of honor. The venerable 70-year-old was en route to a new job as coach at the College of the Pacific in Stockton, California.

Stagg was also spearheading a grass roots movement called "The Drys," fighting the repeal of prohibition by seeking to have prohibition legalized, one neighborhood at a time.

The luncheon was a showcase for The Drys and brought together leaders in government, religion, social movements and athletics to honor Stagg by expressing their opposition to the consumption of alcohol.

Among those leaders was Ernie Waldorf.

Bishop Waldorf's most notable quality was his genius for diplomacy. He had arranged for Tug Wilson to be in attendance, ostensibly to make a speech in favor of prohibition, but Wilson didn't realize he was about to become part of a fortuitous accident.

When Wilson entered the banquet room, he was shown to a seat along the dais next to the 270-pound bishop, who greeted

Tug cordially. Ernie quickly raised the issue Wilson sensed was his purpose for being there. The charismatic clergyman told the athletic director about his son, Lynn, whom he believed was going to be a great football coach.

Ernie encouraged Tug to look into Lynn's record. Wilson, in the context of the situation, took Bishop Waldorf's comment as a direct order from a most important constituency at NU.

The football puzzle, Wilson assumed, was supposed to be solved simply enough: Dick Hanley would not serve out his contract, and in time, Lynn Waldorf would come to Evanston.

Tug thus began inquiring about the bishop's son.

By 1935, Waldorf could no longer resist the lure of Big Ten football, and with his father's quiet intervention, he accepted the coaching job at Northwestern.

That first season in Evanston, incidentally, produced the incident that led to Waldorf's famous nickname. The football world would soon enough come to know a man named Pappy.

Lynn hand-picked Burt Ingwersen for the key position of line coach. Ingwersen was older, more experienced and had been head coach at Iowa from 1924-31.

Burt had resigned from Iowa after the 1931 season, then was quickly hired by Biff Jones as the line coach at Louisiana State. Four successful seasons in Baton Rouge followed, and during that time, Ingwersen acquired an appreciation of bayou culture and affected a Southern accent.

Unfortunately for LSU's coaches, Louisiana Governor Huey Long's meddling in the university's football program had become intolerable, eventually causing both Jones and Ingwersen to resign. And so Burt joined Waldorf's first staff at Northwestern.

Among the coaching luminaries Waldorf had met at the University of Kansas clinic in 1928 was Illinois coach Bob Zuppke. Zuppke had coached Red Grange, but he was also an innovator who introduced and perfected offensive systems such as the deep snap from center, the screen play and the offensive huddle.

When Waldorf assessed his first Northwestern team, he decided the players were decent, but not overwhelming. So he dusted off a strategy he had learned from Zuppke.

"I'll always remember his advice," Waldorf said. "He told me, 'When you're faced with one of those years when your material is only fair and you're not going to win many games, put your eggs in one basket. Pick a tough team and lay for it. Knock it off, and you've got yourself a season.'

"That's exactly what I did my first year at Northwestern. The target I chose was Notre Dame."

Aiming for single upset victory is no easy task, but fortunately for Waldorf, he had on hand Litz Rusness, a holdover from the previous NU coaching regime.

Hanley had respected Rusness' ability to distill masses of information into a concise report on what was required to beat an opponent, but he didn't trust Litz to assist in devising strategy. Dick had the impression Litz owed his loyalty to Tug Wilson, and if he attended staff meetings, Litz would be a pipeline to the athletic director's office.

Wilson had introduced motion pictures to Northwestern's football program in 1929 as the latest technology in teaching and coaching aids.

Since Dick Hanley had little inclination toward intensive film study, Rusness became the first of the football staff to use movies as a strategic device. He developed a method of charting the action, then organizing pages of notes and diagrams to uncover a team's flaws and arriving at conclusions about their strengths and weaknesses.

Rusness spent countless off-season hours breaking down films of every Big Ten game he could get his hands on. Early in his scouting career, he came to the conclusion that the best teams ran successful plays repeatedly. Their basic strategy from game to game was not altered and essentially relied on a high level of execution.

By the end of the 1934 season, Rusness had seen definite new trends in Big Ten football. Coaches had always been aware of their athletes' footspeed, but few of them devised strategies to make the most of that speed.

However, several Big Ten coaches — most notably Minnesota's Bernie Bierman and Ohio State's Francis "Close the Gates of Mercy" Schmidt — had developed innovative ways to feature their swiftest athletes, plays like shovel passes, laterals, reverses and forward passes.

These coaches had stretched defenses horizontally and now were beginning to stretch them vertically. Defensive football, on the other hand, remained relatively constant, since the "Iron Man" substitution rules led coaches to emphasize the offensive part of the game.

Teams typically lined up in one defensive formation. Then, with slight shifting, they stayed in that same scheme for entire games.

Rusness wondered why the element of surprise couldn't be added to the defensive side of the ball. It was a good idea, but it would have to wait, since Hanley wasn't receptive to it.

When Waldorf arrived on the scene, however, Litz Rusness found a sympathetic ear.

During his first decade of coaching, Waldorf often pondered ways of analyzing football games, hoping to isolate key statistical factors that separated winning from losing. However, limited resources and small staffs at Oklahoma City and Oklahoma A&M prevented him from gathering complete information, and the season Lynn was at Kansas State was too short to arrive at any conclusions.

Waldorf had heard of Rusness' film study and looked forward to meeting Litz and hearing about his ideas. Yet when Rusness first walked into Waldorf's small office at Patten Gym, Lynn thought a judge was paying him a visit. He wasn't far off, for the stately looking Rusness' full-time occupation was justice of the peace in Evanston's Municipal Court.

They discussed Rusness' new idea: changing defenses each play.

Litz began by saying, "It's not really changing defenses, although to the other team it would look like the defense changed. The idea is to make your defensive formations flexible enough to shift, countering any last-second changes by the offense."

"How would players know when and how to change?" asked Waldorf.

"The key," answered Rusness, "would be to watch how the backs are placed. That'll tell you what holes they're going to attack and who's liable to throw a pass. All of this can be learned beforehand, because your best teams do it by the numbers; these numbers are like a code, and any code can be broken."

Waldorf inquired, "Since you've thought of everything, how would the changes be communicated to the players, with the rules of the game being what they are?"

Litz replied, "The same way your dad did when he played baseball - with hand signals."

Waldorf quickly realized Litz was a master football strategist. Lynn and his staff began to implement Rusness' new ideas on defense. This was the edge Northwestern would enjoy when the Wildcats later played their "target" game against Notre Dame.

Meanwhile, Waldorf's style of coaching was a breath of fresh air to the returning varsity regulars from Camp Hanley. When Lynn first addressed the team, the new coach of the Wildcats came across as a father or kindly professor, rather than as the scolding schoolmaster who preceded him.

Waldorf stressed that playing on a college football team was only part of the total educational experience a university offers, and players were at school primarily to get an education. In addition, he told them the door to his office was always open.

He invited players to discuss their courses with him and he saw to it there were no conflicts between practices and classes. His players were allowed to miss practices or games if their studies required it.

Then Lynn told them that preparing for a football season was a race against time. He explained that in the 60 minutes of a football game, there really are only 12 to 15 minutes of action, and that, of all team sports, football has the least number of plays per contest.

The coach also mentioned that their team would have 135 hours on the practice field to prepare for a relatively small number of opportunities to succeed. Therefore, they should not waste time or chances.

In his later years, Waldorf spoke of the race against time when he said, "A football season is played to a short, strict schedule. The games are played with a clock looking over your shoulder and during every practice, coaches pray, 'Lord, just give me 10 more minutes.' "

When Northwestern hosted Purdue in the first night football game in Big Ten history, the Boilermakers took a 7-0 lead by returning a punt for a touchdown.

Following the kickoff, the Wildcats steadily marched down to Purdue's 2-yard line. With first and goal to go, the ball was snapped to sophomore fullback Fred Vanzo, who fumbled just as he was about to score.

Purdue recovered the ball and went on to win by that same 7-0 margin.

The targeted showdown came on November 9, and it set up perfectly for Waldorf, since Notre Dame was coming off a stunning 18-13 upset of a supposedly unbeatable Ohio State juggernaut.

Coach Elmer Layden's Irish lost a couple of stars to injury

against Ohio State, halfback Andy Pilney and fullback Fred Cardeo. But Notre Dame boasted passing and punting sensation William Shakespeare - yes, a direct descendant of the English playwright.

This chain of events set up one of the most literary matchups in college football: Shakespeare against Northwestern end Henry Wadsworth Longfellow.

Unfortunately for the Cats, while Longfellow was a great defensive player, he couldn't catch a pass on offense. Waldorf worked patiently with this talented kid who couldn't seem to clear a psychological hurdle.

"Catch the ball with your hands, Henry," Waldorf preached. "Two hands working together, Henry."

Finally, with tension building and the Notre Dame matchup just days away, Waldorf did two things simultaneously, each of which was unbelievably rare for him. He lost his temper and he cursed.

Longfellow dropped yet another pass and the entire Northwestern team almost went into shock when Waldorf screamed, "God damn it, Henry. Just once can't you catch the damn ball?"

That was the end of practice.

Bring on Notre Dame.

Wildcat hopes were anything but bright when game day arrived it was pouring rain in Notre Dame Stadium. After the Irish ran a half-dozen plays, Northwestern made the game's first substitution.

When Al Lind went into the game replacing Sammy Wegner at center, it attracted little notice. This was Northwestern's most important tactical move, though, because Lind had been trained to use the hand signals that would change NU's defensive alignment on each play. He sat on the bench during the early minutes of the contest to observe which holes the Fighting Irish offense attacked.

After entering the game, Al chose the defense for each upcoming play once he'd noted where Notre Dame's wingback, quarterback and fullback had positioned themselves.

Northwestern's players didn't huddle when they were on defense, but their defensive linemen and linebackers would line up in a 5-3 formation until the Irish backfield shifted. Then, after Lind flashed a signal, a different linebacker would move into a down position to form one of three schemes - a "Regular Six," "Overshifted Six," or "Tight Six."

At times, the Cats remained in their basic 5-3 defense. Because the schemes operated via hand signals and most of the alignments had six-man lines, Waldorf called it his "Secret Six Defense."

As the grueling afternoon wore on, the Northwestern defense continue to befuddle Notre Dame's attack.

As for Longfellow, Henry made two huge plays as Northwestern scored a 14-7 upset in a game which propelled Waldorf to national Coach of the Year honors.

Longfellow caught a touchdown pass from Wallie Cruice for the Wildcats first score - leaping above Shakespeare, among others, for the reception - and recovered a critical third-quarter fumble.

A newspaper photo of Henry's TD catch the following day carried this unforgettable caption: "Longfellow Murders Shakespeare!"

Northwestern's coaches and their wives went out to celebrate the historic victory that night, and were surprised to find Waldorf oddly distracted. Line coach Burt Ingwersen asked if anything was wrong.

"Nothing's wrong," Waldorf said. "It's just that I'm worried about a letdown. I'm wondering how we're going to get the boys ready for Wisconsin."

"Aw, Lynn," drawled Burt, "You should be kickin' up your heels and here you are sittin' there. Carryin' it all on your shoulders, lookin' out for everybody, worryin' your hair gray.

"Remember when they took us to that nightclub a few months ago and all those guys started dancin' with the hostesses? You just sat there nursin' a drink and that ol' boy kept callin' you an ol' pappy.

"How'd you like it if we started callin' you 'Pappy'?"

And the name stuck.

A footnote to the 1935 season: As one of his rewards for the national coaching honor, Waldorf's picture appeared on boxes of Wheaties breakfast cereal.

"Unfortunately, General Mills didn't send me any cash. Instead, they sent cases of that breakfast food to our house," Waldorf said. "I got tired of eating Wheaties, Louise got tired of Wheaties, our two daughters got tired of Wheaties and even our dog Pixie got tired of Wheaties."

One year later, Pappy was the toast of the coaching world.

It was also during this period that Lynn began a friendship with poet Carl Sandburg. Sandburg was in the process of finishing his six-volume biography of Abraham Lincoln, and enlisted Waldorf's help because the author lacked insight on the Civil War.

Lynn was extremely well-versed on the subject, especially the Reconstruction Period. He and Sandburg met at the Waldorf home in Wilmette for long sessions lasting well into the night.

The result was a volume entitled "Abraham Lincoln: The War Years." After the book was published in 1939, Sandburg presented a copy to Lynn, which the author inscribed, "To Lynn Waldorf. With affectionate good wishes, Carl Sandburg."

In Waldorf's second season at Northwestern, the varsity was bolstered by the addition of two talented teen-agers, 19-year-old tackle Bob Voigts from Evanston and 18-year-old halfback Bernie Jefferson, an African-American from Grand Rapids, Michigan.

As a student at Evanston Township High, Voigts showed exceptional athletic talent and played on six championship teams — two each in football, basketball and baseball. In his senior year, the football team had an 8-0 record, scoring 142 points and giving up only 12. Bob was named All-State that year, a rare achievement at that time for a player from a Chicago suburban high school.

Even with Voigts and Jefferson joining the team, however, winning a conference title was a tall order, because the Wildcats entered that season with Don Heap as their lone left halfback, meaning that anyone substituting for Heap would be playing out of position.

The most noticeable change from 1935 was the shift of Fred Vanzo from fullback to blocking back. Vanzo was the young man who had become disconsolate when his fumble lost the Purdue game a year earlier, but Waldorf's relentless support kept Vanzo's head up.

Minnesota and Ohio State, teams with the nation's most wide-open offenses, were co-favorites in the Big Ten that year.

Bernie Bierman's Minnesota team featured his innovative "buck lateral," which sports writers deemed unstoppable. As for Ohio State, coach Francis Schmidt had crafted a wild and woolly "Scarlet Scourge" offense that sometimes called for five laterals on a single play.

In the fourth quarter of their game with Ohio State, Northwestern lined up in a formation no one had ever seen before — an unbalanced line with two tackles and the quarterback just to the right of the center, left end Johnny Kovatch standing a yard off the line of scrimmage in a wing position and right half Don Geyer a yard off the line in a gap between the right tackle and right end.

Waldorf called it "The Cockeyed Formation," but in fact, it became football's first slot formation and it gave tailback Heap four targets in the days when most teams sent out only two receivers.

Heap connected with Kovatch on a 42-yard gainer. Three plays later, Heap scored from five yards out and Northwestern had scrambled to a 14-13 victory.

Ohio State attempted to mount a comeback, but the threat ended when Williams' pass was intercepted at NU's 7-yard line.

That cardiac comeback injected NU with the confidence they needed to take on Minnesota, which had used the infamous "buck lateral" to score four touchdowns in its previous two games.

Halloween afternoon, 1936, was Northwestern's first home sellout in six years, and Pappy had a trick planned for the Gophers — yet another defensive wrinkle in which a tackle would not charge from the line of scrimmage. This was the first attempt at "read and react" defense, and it also involved elements of what now is known as the zone blitz.

Minnesota came to Evanston with a 28-game unbeaten streak, and hundreds of sports writers from coast to coast were present to chronicle the momentous collision. In addition, there were nine radio hookups, including the CBS and NBC national networks.

On Minnesota's second play, Andy Uram broke loose on the buck lateral as Northwestern blew its special coverage. Uram should have scored, but he slipped on the rain-soaked field and went out of bounds at the Wildcat 23-yard line.

Ultimately, the Gophers got nothing when a fake field goal went awry and the game stayed scoreless at halftime.

Early in the third quarter, Northwestern was backed up to its own 1-yard line. Waldorf recalled what happened next: "Our punter was Bernard Jefferson, an 18-year-old who had never, during his short competition in college football, had to kick from behind the goal line, and I wondered how he was going to react.

"It was raining, the ball was wet, and a wet ball can drill through a punter's hands for a fumble very easily. There were those seven Minnesota linemen; they were really big, and they could rush a punter.

"Well, Jefferson calmly kicked a beautiful punt 50 yards downfield. I breathed a sigh of relief. I believe from that instant he was a better football player. He passed the test under fire. After that game, we began calling him 'Big Jeff.' "

The teams slogged back and forth on the soggy field, until Northwestern arrived at a second-and-goal situation on Minnesota's 1-yard line.

Steve Toth's second-down smash couldn't budge the Gopher defense, but, on the next play, Fred Vanzo's lead block created a gap just wide enough to get Toth through for the touchdown.

The NU players didn't even try to talk to each other because the crowd was yelling so loud. It was only the second touchdown Minnesota had given up that season.

Toth's PAT attempt was blocked by Ray Antil, Northwestern had taken a 6-0 lead.

Years later, Pappy described the final minutes of that game, saying, "There were five minutes to go, Minnesota had the ball on their 20-yard line and called for an off-tackle play. Uram came off tackle.

"Vanzo, who had been in all 55 minutes, was in at the right side to tackle him. Just as he was tackling Uram, he flipped the ball to (Rudy) Gmitro, their fastest man. Gmitro, in the 100-yard dash, could beat Vanzo by 10 yards.

"Our films showed that, as Vanzo was coming up on his knees after making the hit on Uram, Gmitro was six yards down the field, and yet 40 yards further down the field, just as Gmitro dodged our safety and had a clear field for a touchdown, it was Vanzo who caught him from behind. How he got there, I will never know.

"After 55 minutes of awfully hard football, as hard as any boy ever played, he had the courage to get up and go after what seemed to be the impossible, and it saved the game for us."

Despite the Gophers' remarkable rushing statistics on a muddy track of 256 yards on 36 carries, an average of 7.1 yards per rush, they had been shut out. Their four-year unbeaten streak had come to an end.

"I think most of all, I'll remember that group as a whole," Waldorf said. "I can honestly say I would have been just as proud of them even if we had lost. I told them afterward, I hoped the experience they had of uniting with a common goal and winning that game was something they each could have again, individually, in more important things later on.

"Then Bernie Bierman walked in. He shook my hand and said, 'I want to say, you have a splendidly coached team, Lynn. As long as we had to lose, I would rather lose to you than anybody.'

"His gesture taught me something. It's easy to congratulate your opponent when you're the victor, but it takes a lot of inner strength to be the first one to shake the hand of the winner when you're the loser."

There was talk among the public and in print about the Wildcats running the table and winning the national championship, but it wasn't to be.

Northwestern lost its season finale at Notre Dame, 26-6.

Neverthless, as a bonus for winning the Big Ten title, Lynn, Louise and their daughters were invited to San Francisco by the organizers of the East-West Shrine Game. Lynn's official duty was to serve as the Big Ten's observer.

The Waldorfs fell in love with northern California, and as Pappy recalled years later, "After that, I always had it in the back of my mind that if a job in California or Washington ever opened up, I'd take it."

The following season, Northwestern suffered a heartbreaking 7-0 loss to Ohio State, but it helped one Wildcat learn a valuable lesson.

At a critical point in the game, Bernie Jefferson dropped back to punt. He was supposed to kick down the middle of the field, but at the last minute, decided to kick to his left and stepped outside his blockers before he booted the ball.

As Pappy recalled, "Ohio State's right tackle, Carl Kaplanoff, came in and blocked the kick because Big Jeff had left his cup of protection. That resulted in the game's only score. He took it really hard, but I told him that we should look at it as a positive learning experience.

"The lesson was that the punt is such an important play that a punter should always stay within his protection and let his blockers do their job the way they were taught to do it. You have to trust your supporting cast. Let them do their jobs so you can do your job."

Chapter 3

The following Saturday at Wisconsin, Pappy learned a lesson himself, when he became so absorbed in NU's 14-6 victory that he forgot about his pipe burning, and it singed a hole in his suit pocket.

A football coach must keep up appearances, and that wouldn't do. So Pappy first switched to chain-smoking cigarettes, then later to the big cigars that became his trademark.

That '37 season also marked the end of the prep football career of the hottest recruiting prospect from that era, Bill DeCorrevont of Chicago's Austin High. DeCorrevont scored at least one touchdown in every game during his four years of high school football and during that 1937 season, he scored an almost unbelievable 218 points in 11 games.

DeCorrevont and six of his Austin High teammates chose Northwestern, and he was the first prep star to announce his choice of college coast-to-coast on a live NBC radio broadcast.

Northwestern's varsity also was bolstered by the addition of Joe Lokanc in 1938. He and Hal Method, who preceded him by a year, were talented young linemen from East Chicago, Indiana, brought to the Evanston campus by NU assistant athletic director Ade Schumacher. Joe had played prep ball at Washington High, while Hal had played at Roosevelt High.

Lokanc had been an Indiana state heavyweight wrestling champion, and that experience was a tremendous help to his development as a football player.

Lokanc blossomed as a guard under Burt Ingwersen and remembers his line coach as having "an uncanny ability to tell which of his linemen were ready to play by watching them in warmups." Because of that, Pappy gave Burt complete authority to make line substitutions.

Waldorf was involved in another remarkable tale in 1938. The legendary Amos Alonzo Stagg, then 76 and still coaching at College of the Pacific, was driving cross-country to visit relatives in the East when he decided to stop and tour the University of Notre Dame.

Elmer Layden, ND's athletic director and head football coach, upon hearing that Stagg was on campus, rushed over to greet "The Grand Old Man."

In the course of their conversation, Layden told Stagg of plans to hold the world premiere of the movie about Knute Rockne right there in South Bend during the first week of October, 1940.

Layden proposed that Stagg's Pacific team play Notre Dame that weekend as part of the festivities, and Stagg accepted.

Playing a nationally-known football power would give the small Methodist college in Stockton, California tremendous exposure, but it also exposed the school's minuscule athletic budget. Stagg needed as much scouting information as he could get in order for his team to give the Irish any kind of a game, but Pacific's lack of cash prohibited any scouting trips to the Midwest.

So the old coach dipped into his football espionage fund, a cigar box full of three-cent stamps, and fired off an SOS to another coach of a Methodist school that faced Notre Dame every year — Lynn Waldorf.

Stagg asked to borrow NU's game film after Northwestern played Notre Dame in 1939. Pappy answered the letter with a long distance call and told Pacific's coach, "I'll see to it you'll be sent not only our film, but all of our scouting reports immediately after we play 'em."

Stagg thanked Lynn, but said, "Just the movie will do. I like to see things for myself."

After the 1939 season ended, a package arrived at Stagg's home in Stockton that loaded the coach's off-season plate. It contained not only a film of the Northwestern-Notre Dame game, but seven other 1939 Fighting Irish games - practically the entire season.

Stagg made good use of the celluloid. In October of 1940, his team traveled to South Bend played Notre Dame to a 7-7 halftime tie, before being owered in the second half and losing, 25-7.

Pacific came up short on the board, but retained a ton of dignity.

When the story surfaced that S had the advantage of all those Notre Dame films, and Layd s asked about Waldorf's involvement, he just smiled and 'I'm glad Stagg's team gave my men a tough game. It he them get ready for a tough season. What Lynn did was th thing to do."

No one, however, bothered to ask how Waldorf got all the movies.

Pappy had done what all good researchers do. He went to the source - in this case, the Notre Dame football coach. Layden was the same coach who would bring his players down a peg by delivering blows to their egos in his column, which appeared regularly in the *South Bend Tribune.*

Layden wasn't averse to helping an overmatched, but respected opponent scout his Notre Dame team in order to teach his athletes a lesson.

By 1939, Northwestern had enjoyed five seasons of huge gate receipts. Pappy and athletic director Tug Wilson were able to offer Wes Fry a head coach's salary to leave Kansas State and become Waldorf's chief assistant.

While at K-State, Fry had set off offensive fireworks in the Big Six, and his squad shattered the school's single-game scoring record when by racking up 47 points against Iowa State.

During a rainy 1936 game against Oklahoma A&M, Fry's Wildcats had pulled off an exotic "Sleeper Play" in which a halfback came out from behind the umpire, who was holding an umbrella, to catch a touchdown pass.

Fry's five-year coaching record in Manhattan of 18-21-6 doesn't appear impressive, but his winning percentage of .467 was unsurpassed by any K-State head coach until Bill Snyder's magnificent rebuilding job in the 1990s.

With the addition of DeCorrevont and Alf Bauman to the roster, Northwestern was ranked No. 1 in the 1939 preseason polls. NU, however, got off to a horrendous start that year, losing to Oklahoma and Ohio State by a combined score of 36-0.

Years later, Pappy recalled, "Unfortunately, DeCorrevont was hurt just when he was getting started. That's why he did not play more for us that first year. If Bill had been himself, we would have scored more points."

During another game that year, Lokanc and Bauman discovered that Waldorf enjoyed seeing his players express creativity by contributing their ideas to the team's strategy.

Bauman was so strong, he normally could fire off the line defensively and smash through anything in his path. The opposition, though, began to trap-block him to slow him down, so Lokanc said to Alfie, "Don't worry about those traps. Just tie up the interference. I'll follow you and make the tackle."

Their improvised defensive stunt worked well. Lokanc nailed ball carriers for losses and the duo closed down their side of the field. After they went to the sidelines, Pappy asked them what they had been doing. When the two players explained, Waldorf said, "As long as you have a good reason for what you do, fine. Just keep the pressure on."

The Waldorf years at Northwestern became a time when the Big Ten's most competitive rivalry was NU against Minnesota.

From 1935-41, those games resulted in four wins for Minnesota and three for Northwestern — with a one-point total cumulative difference, 59-58 for Minnesota.

These were the years Bernie Bierman fielded America's most dominant squads, winning five conference titles and three national championships.

The most memorable game between the two schools was the 1941 duel in Minneapolis. Twenty-four men on the field that day went on to play in the National Football League.

In the middle of the third quarter, DeCorrevont took a wallop. Still somewhat disoriented and with blood streaming from his nose, he dropped back to punt on fourth down from his own 26.

Ed Lechner put on a hard rush and partially blocked the kick. The ball bounced out of bounds at Northwestern's 41-yard line.

Minnesota called time out, and during a break in the action, Bierman informed referee John Getchell that a special play Bierman had told him about before the game would be the second play run after play resumed.

On first down, 153-pound halfback Bud Higgins reversed the ball to Bob Swieger, who was swarmed by four Wildcats and dropped for no gain. As the gang unpiled, Sweiger began talking to the NU players.

Before Northwestern realized what was happening, Minnesota lined up without a huddle in a strange formation. Six Gopher linemen were to the right of the ball, with center Gene Flick at the end of the line in the spot normally occupied by the left end. Flick, who was also a pitcher on the Gophers' baseball team, didn't drop into his usual four-point stance, but quickly snapped the ball and tossed it in a sidearm motion back to Bud Higgins.

Higgins took off around the right end and romped 41 yards for a touchdown. The play that scored the winning points in Minnesota's 8-7 victory became known as "The Talking Play."

Bierman had shown it to his squad at a secret Friday afternoon practice. It was such a secret that he had it snipped from the game film afterward.

John Haman earned All-American honors as a result of his heroics during the 1939 season. Hal Method, the East Chicago lineman and pre-med student, played in the Blue-Gray Game that year.

Method's last game was the 1940 College All-Star contest, for which the squad was chosen by millions of football fans casting ballots printed in newspapers across the country.

Santa Clara's Buck Shaw, Princeton's Tad Wieman and Iowa's Dr. Eddie Anderson coached for the collegians in the annual classic against the NFL champs. Waldorf was an unofficial member of their staff, since Northwestern always hosted the All-Stars.

An injury to one of the elected tackles, however, resulted in the last-minute addition of Lee Artoe to the roster. A 6-foot-3, 225-pound tackle, Artoe was on the Santa Clara 1937 Sugar Bowl champion team before transferring to the University of California and earning a bachelor of science in chemistry.

Waldorf met Artoe when Lee's train arrived at Chicago's Union Station. During the drive to the NU campus, Artoe amazed Waldorf when he confided that he never practiced when he played at Cal. Attending practices was impossible given his work schedule. To get through school, Lee worked a midnight to 6:30 a.m. shift at a Texaco gas station near Oakland.

Artoe and Waldorf became close during the weeks of preparation for the match against the Green Bay Packers. The All-Star coaches discovered that, in addition to his fast, low charge off the line, Artoe could keep pace with receivers. They decided to use him to foil the NFL's most explosive passing attack - Cecil Isbell to Don Hutson.

Early in the first quarter, USC's star back Ambrose Schindler intercepted Isbell at the Packers' 18-yard line. The All-Stars scored a touchdown in three plays, with Schindler carrying on each snap.

On Green Bay's next play from their 35-yard line, Isbell threw to Hutson, but Artoe jostled the Hall of Fame receiver, preventing a completion. On the next play, Lee broke through and nailed Isbell for a 16-yard loss.

However, when the Packers left their huddle on third down, Hutson split 30 yards away from the interior linemen, so Artoe looked to the coaches for guidance. Buck Shaw signaled him to line up inside but Wieman waved him to get out with Hutson.

Waldorf just stood on the sidelines between Shaw and Wieman, with his arms crossed and a pained look on his face. Pappy couldn't say anything because he was an "unofficial" assistant coach.

The coaches' final decision has long since been forgotten. However, records of the game show on the next play, Isbell connected with Hutson for an 81-yard touchdown pass and the Packers eventually beat the collegians, 45-28.

Lee Artoe went on the become a star with the Chicago Bears as a tackle and, surprisingly, Artoe had a magic toe. He once booted a 52-yard field goal in those leather-helmet NFL days. Lee was on the 1940 world championship squad, and later played for the Los Angeles Dons in the upstart AFC.

Artoe later fashioned a successful business career, but he never forgot the people who helped him along the way. He became a force in the National Football League Players Association (NFLPA). Through his efforts, pre-1959 players attained full-fledged membership in the union's pension plan.

In May of 1999, Lee Artoe was honored with the NFLPA Award For Courage for "... being the first to provide his fellow players with an alternative to being ensnared in the NFL's old restricted system."

Lee Artoe was the pioneer of free agency.

Northwestern opened their 1940 season with a road game against Pappy's alma mater, Syracuse - a glorious homecoming for Louise and Lynn, as NU's Wildcats romped, 40-0.

The Wildcats finished the season with a 6-2 mark. The highlight was a 20-0 win over Notre Dame. Only narrow losses to Minnesota and Michigan by a combined margin of eight points kept Northwestern from a Big Ten title.

Waldorf's success at Northwestern was amazing because he was forced to work with small squads. As Pappy said, "Overall, things were uneven at Northwestern. We were never able to offer as much financial aid as we were allowed to under the rules."

High tuition and stringent entrance requirements prevented Northwestern from having large rosters. In addition, the Big Ten rule against freshman football games made it difficult for Waldorf and his staff to develop young players.

Luckily, Northwestern's players generally came from well-organized high school football programs and were well-grounded in fundamentals.

NCAA rules first allowed "two-platoon football" in 1941, and Northwestern took advantage of the rule change, as the Wildcats' roster swelled to 65 players. However, Pappy found it difficult to take advantage of the two-platoon rule, because the team faced a new hindrance when NU changed to a quarter system of classes.

The new routine of classes and labs allowed for the entire team to practice together only twice a week.

Also that year, the Wildcats welcomed a truly special sophomore halfback - Otto Graham of nearby Waukegan.

Northwestern kicked off its 1941 season against Kansas State in Dyche Stadium, and Graham's college career was launched when he returned a punt 94 yards for a touchdown in NU's 51-0 blowout win.

Graham did double duty that day, as he would for all of Northwestern's home games. Since he was on a band scholarship, he quickly changed from football gear to band uniform, played and marched during halftime, then changed back into his pads for the second half of the game.

With all of their problems, disappointments and unpleasant surprises, Northwestern still finished 5-3 that year. NU handed Paul Brown's Ohio State squad its only loss, and that same group of Buckeyes were national champions the following year.

The Wildcats' three losses were to the nation's first, third and fifth-ranked teams by a combined margin of only nine points.

The end of the 1941 season also signaled the start of America's involvement in World War II, and the war had a strange effect on football. Before Pearl Harbor was attacked, unstable conditions worldwide had led Northwestern's administrators to consider how the university would cope in the event of hostilities. In addition, they determined which school resources might be devoted to the nation's war effort.

By June of 1942, Northwestern was hosting various training programs for military and homefront support.

Regarding the football program, while it was determined that NU would still field a team, Waldorf and his staff were unable to conduct spring practice. The Big Ten was encouraged by the Department of the Navy to continue playing football for the sake of morale of the men in uniform, whether they attended games or listened to broadcasts over Armed Services Radio. Schedules were increased from eight to 10 games.

The war created a manpower shortage, though, which prompted the relaxation of eligibility rules. Under the new rules, freshmen were allowed to compete on varsities, competition during the war did not count against eligibility, and two Midwestern service squads, the Iowa Pre-Flight Seahawks and the Great Lakes Bluejackets from just north of Chicago, were added to Big Ten schedules.

The Seahawks and Bluejackets were allowed to stock their rosters with former high school, college and even pro football players. In addition to being terribly overmatched by service teams, college coaches faced an epidemic of inconsistency resulting from the questionable status of players, who could be drafted at any time during the season. In addition, schools with Army ROTC programs weren't allowed to use military trainees as players and were reduced to playing 4-Fs (men considered unfit for military service) and freshmen. Between the stress and competitive imbalance, many schools decided fielding a team was too difficult and simply suspended football for the duration of the war.

It was a miracle Northwestern even had a team. But the Wildcats faced a difficult 10-game schedule with only four returning starters. Military induction had drained the Wildcats of talent, and the only returning regulars were players enrolled in the NROTC program carrying B-averages or better.

Fortunately, Otto Graham was part of that group. But as an additional handicap, most players had attended only five workouts before the season began.

NU's only win that season was a 3-0 squeaker over the University of Texas. Longtime bench warmer Allen Pick kicked a 22-yard field goal to decide it.

Reflecting on that season, Pappy said, "The biggest lesson I learned in that losing season was a new respect for the young men who play football. The winning team has a great incentive, but I believe a losing season demands more moral stamina and genuine courage from the gang. Never once did they quit, and perhaps the most notable quality of those boys was their resiliency.

"It was encouraging, too, when I'd hear from past players who were in the armed services. They'd tell me how much football meant to them and how much they enjoyed the game.

"That 1942 Northwestern squad was also my first great passing team. This was because of Otto Graham, who had big hands, good ball control and truly remarkable eyes. Otto could observe all sections of the field at once, pick his man coolly and time his passes accurately.

"Our pet play was run from the Single Wing, called "Number One Pass." We'd pull both guards and roll the tailback out to the right, where he could either run or pass. It put a strain on the left defensive halfback, who'd have to watch for the running threat, and if the defense rotated, both ends were open for passes.

"Otto Graham completed 16 passes against Michigan using that very play. In that game, he was 20 out of 29 for 310 yards."

During that 1942 season, Otto Graham shattered NU records records by attempting 182 passes and completing 89 for 1,092 yards, numbers which were also Big Ten milestones.

The war and its travel restrictions, combined with the fact that most ex-collegians and pro football players had been called to active duty, threatened to end the College All-Star Game.

However, Tug Wilson and Pappy Waldorf devised a plan to save the annual classic. They gained the full cooperation of the armed services by arranging rent-free use of Dyche Stadium in 1943 and 1944 for the event, thereby channeling all receipts to a servicemen's fund.

As a result, transportation and leave time were provided for both pro champions and former college standouts. The 1943 game produced more revenue than any of its predecessors, every penny of which went to the Chicago Servicemen's Centers.

The Washington Redskins appeared touchdown-bound midway through the third quarter of that game, but when Sammy Baugh tried to pass from the collegians' 18-yard line, Otto Graham intercepted the throw.

Graham snatched the ball on his 3-yard line, dodged into the clear, swerved to the left and raced 97 yards for a touchdown which was the turning point in the All-Stars' 27-7 victory.

Looking back, Pappy said, "I guess I was fortunate during those years just to have a football team. We were primarily a service team. I don't think there were a dozen on the squad who were civilians, and most of them were freshmen under 18. The rest were Navy and Marine officer candidates. How long I had them and how much I could use them was completely out of my hands."

The Wildcats lost most of the 1942 squad through graduation or military duty, but they were bolstered by an impressive array of transfer students assigned to NU's V-12 program. A 6-2 record was the result in 1943.

Graham scored 27 points against Wisconsin that year, which remains the school's single-game scoring record. NU missed out on a share of the Big Ten title by a single game.

Waldorf's varsity roster for the 1944 season consisted of 51 players — 43 of them freshmen who would have been the pride and joy of any coaching staff in peacetime. But accelerated curricula and lack of spring practice put them on the firing line with only a few weeks of summer drills behind them. Under the circumstances, it was a monumental achievement just to field a team and play a full schedule. Northwestern played 10 games, managed to win one and played Minnesota to a 14-14 tie.

During this time, Pappy and Wes Fry became regulars at Chicago Bears home games, primarily to study the Bears version of the T-Formation. They knew the deception offered by that offensive strategy would be popular in post-World War II football.

NU's coaches saw that, in addition to enhancing the quarterback position, it was also effective with halfbacks who had quick first steps and with fullbacks who could accurately throw passes.

"The Chicago Bears co-head coach Luke Johnsos, who was also

a Northwestern alum, graciously volunteered to help Wes and me install the T-Formation during spring practice in 1945," Waldorf said. "But we didn't adopt the same 'Man-in-Motion T' used by the Bears. Our version featured single-wing shoulder blocking. We wanted to move defenders on the edge of the defense out of the way to make the most of our halfbacks' ability to get a quick start.

"We developed a play called '42 Crossfire,' which accomplished this. It was a counter play, with the left half carrying off right tackle. The keys to this play were the quarterback making a good fake to the fullback and the right guard pulling out to block the man on the defense's perimeter."

Waldorf also hired Bob Tessier in 1946. As well as being a superb teacher of line play, Tessier contributed fresh ideas to strategy sessions, especially when defense was discussed. Tessier was an advocate of "stunting" defensive tactics, in which linebackers and linemen exchange rushing lanes.

Unfortunately, Northwestern had so many new faces on the team in 1946, Tessier's defensive schemes could not be used often.

Concerning the NCAA's football eligibility rules, 1946 was considered a war year, so freshmen were allowed to play on varsities. To ease the transition of war vets into Big Ten competition, the league decreed for that season only, fall practice be expanded from three weeks, three days to five full weeks.

Northwestern had the largest number of players trying out for the team in their history.

Loran "Pee Wee" Day remembered that there was something very different about those fall drills.

"The night before practice started," Pee Wee said, "everyone trying out for the team — must have been 160 men or so — gathered in the main ballroom of the North Shore Hotel and were seated at long tables. We each stood up and introduced ourselves.

"The next day, not one coach missed calling any player by their correct first name."

Alex Sarkisian was an unofficial recruiter as well as a varsity football player that year. Fellow East Chicago players Art Murakowski and Ed Nemeth were going to register at Illinois, but as Alex recalled, "I told them how really easy it was to play for Pappy. They decided to come to Northwestern."

When it came to winning starting positions, Pappy believed players should wait their turn. Out of loyalty to the players who had been with him before war, Waldorf allowed them to retain the starting jobs earned before going into the service. However, if they were injured, they had little chance of reclaiming a starting spot because of the glut of talented newcomers.

Major problems surfaced when Jim Farrar, the team's best passer, was called to active military duty and Ray Justak, an outstanding tackle, was forced to quit football because of the demands of his law studies. Justak's loss, though, was for a good cause - he went on to become the head of the Indiana Parole Board.

During this transitional season, Waldorf often reminded his assistants to be more tolerant of mistakes than they were before the war because, as Pappy put it: "These men have been through a lot of stress and a lot of regimentation."

Although 1946 wasn't a championship season for the Wildcats, it produced several interesting moments.

Northwestern's first opponent was Iowa State. The Cyclones opened their season a week before the Wildcats, so Waldorf was able to personally scout them. However, in the spirit of fair play, Pappy welcomed the Iowa State coach to be present at NU's intrasquad scrimmage.

Northwestern opened the Big Ten portion of its '46 schedule against Minnesota in Dyche Stadium. The Wildcats ran "42 Crossfire" on their first play from scrimmage, and Frank Aschenbrenner exploded 67 yards for a touchdown, his first of two scores that day as NU won, 14-7.

Then the Wildcats traveled to Ann Arbor the following Saturday and played Michigan to a 14-14 draw, a tie which ultimately cost the Wolverines a trip to the Rose Bowl.

NU also played the College of the Pacific in Dyche Stadium that year in honor of Pacific's coach, the legendary Stagg. Before the kickoff, Pappy told the Wildcats, "After you knock 'em down, offer 'em a hand and help pick 'em up. Do that for the Grand Old Man."

Some of Pacific's players, however, took offense at the courtesy. One even kicked Alex Sarkisian on the chin.

After the Wildcats built a 20-0 lead at halftime, Waldorf didn't allow the first or second-string players to take the field for the third quarter. He put his third and fourth-string players into the game.

Recalling that season, Pappy said, "We did very well in our first five games, but we got a few kids hurt and we suffered some losses to Ohio State and Illinois at the end. All in all, it was a pretty fair year."

At the conclusion of the 1946 season, no one, least of all Waldorf, had any idea that the dream he'd tucked away in the back of his mind over a decade earlier was about to come true.

Chapter 4

GOIN' WEST

I t's hard to imagine that there are many institutions of higher learning more renowned than the University of California.

Over the years, 16 members of Cal's faculty have won Nobel Peace Prizes, while in a remarkably different vein, the school always has been a haven for free speech and free thinking.

This philosophy stemmed from its German-style roots. The German university concept meant the institution provided classrooms and laboratories, then left the students on their own, with no residence halls, few intramural athletic fields and minimal provisions for student activities or cultural affairs.

In 1904, Benjamin Ide Wheeler, the school's president, granted the students the right to organize as the Associated Students of the University of California (ASUC), to provide extracurricular activities for the campus. Thus, the University of California was the only school in the country whose football program was completely controlled by its student body.

The ASUC and faculty coexisted harmoniously until 1946, when the football players encountered serious philosophical differences with the coaching staff in general and head coach Frank Wickhorst in particular.

The Bears had endured a horrible 2-7 season, as returning war vets squabbled with younger players and Wickhorst lost control. Tensions mounted as the situation grew more strained with each passing week. By the end of the season, the players felt completely demoralized and decided the time had come to take action.

Meanwhile, students and fans weren't happy, either. They actually tore out sections of seats at Memorial Stadium during the dispiriting, season-ending loss to arch-rival Stanford.

Players Ted Kenfield and Ed Welch drew up and circulated a petition calling for the firing of all the coaches. All but two of 44 varsity signed it. So on Thanksgiving eve — November 27, 1946 — the Executive Committee of ASUC convened and a large audience overflowed the meeting room.

Halfback Bob Dal Porto addressed the committee. He held up the document and said, "The past season has served to bring the athletic situation at the university to a head. The men on the football team lack confidence in the coach. By being pushed around by the coaches, the team lost confidence in themselves and the whole situation caused disorganization and disunity all season.

"It is the consensus of the team that the present coaching staff and the entire athletic management staff should be removed from office."

It was then proposed that Frank Wickhorst and most of his assistants be fired. Two assistants, Nibs Price and Zeb Chaney, who were also the school's basketball coaches, were not included in the proposal.

Less than two weeks later, Welch informed Wickhorst that the committee had voted 7 to 1 for his removal.

The firing of Wickhorst and the majority of his assistants resulted in instant national notoriety for the giant university. UC was ridiculed as a school where students can fire football coaches and a coach's graveyard.

Cal's President, Robert G. Sproul, knew he didn't have the authority to overrule the action, but with his limited power, he immediately took steps to restructure the athletic department, drastically reducing ASUC's clout.

Sproul decreed ASUC would continue to receive football revenue, but no longer would control hiring and firing of coaches.The president also appointed Brutus Hamilton, the university's dean of men and former track coach, as the school's first athletic director.

Hamilton's initial choice as Cal's next football coach was Fritz Crisler, who had been highly successful at Michigan as both coach and athletic director. However, Crisler turned the job down after he flew out for a closer look and realized Cal's football situation was unstable.

On the downside, the world's largest university had bickering alumni, only one booster organization and no recruiting network. Worse still, Cal's players had proven they could be mutinous, and Crisler felt it was unlikely that anybody would be able to coach them.

So the search continued.

Lynn and Louise Waldorf were in New York City in early January of 1947 to attend the annual American Football Coaches Association meetings. While they were in town, they had dinner with Hamilton, who was an old friend of Bishop Ernest Waldorf.

Lynn and Louise first had met Hamilton when he and Lynn were coaches at the University of Kansas. Pappy always referred to Brutus as "... one of the finest gentlemen who ever lived."

During the course of the evening, Hamilton off-handedly asked Waldorf if he might be interested in the job as Cal's football coach. Pappy surprised the athletic director when he replied, "Naturally, I would be."

Pappy told Hamilton he believed the situation at California was not a case of inmates running the asylum. On the contrary, he felt the university was a school with great diversity in a state where students took a healthy interest in the game. Cal was a place where a Rose Bowl team could be built, Waldorf suggested.

Waldorf made it plain he thought Cal was a "slumbering giant," not any kind graveyard.

A month later, Hamilton telephoned Waldorf and asked if he would take the job. Pappy replied that he would consider it. Then, on February 14, Hamilton called again and read Waldorf a rough draft of a coaching contract paying $13,500 per year.

Pappy requested a clause in the contract that stated Pappy would answer only to the president of the university, and that he alone would have the right to hire and fire his assistant coaches.

Hamilton agreed to the changes, and Lynn said he would accept the offer if he could obtain a release from his contract at Northwestern, which had two years remaining.

Later that day, Waldorf met with Northwestern's president, Franklin Bliss Snyder, and asked for the release. The president, who never questioned Waldorf's motives, agreed without hesitation. The following day, Northwestern's athletic board held a special meeting to verify the decision.

While that meeting was in progress, Waldorf met with his Northwestern team to ensure they heard the news from him, rather than reading about it in the paper. Pappy said, "It's best for a coach to make a change every seven to 10 years, because it's almost impossible to have a run last much longer."

After the athletic board approved his release, Pappy phoned Hamilton and officially accepted the job. Then he called Nibs Price and Zeb Chaney at UC and welcomed them to his staff.

In addition to their basketball duties, Price would coach the defensive backs and punters, while Chaney would scout for and coach the Ramblers.

Waldorf took his first trip to Berkeley in February, 1947. His train was met by an impressive group, including Hamilton, Jim Scott of the *Berkeley Gazette*, star lineman Rod Franz and Norrie West, Cal's sports publicity man.

West recalled another person who met that train.

"Marchy Schwartz came over from Palo Alto to greet him. No Stanford coach had ever done that," West said.

Waldorf spoke to a gathering at the Claremont Hotel the evening of his arrival in Berkeley and summarized his plans this way: "I've come to awaken the sleeping giant of the west."

In addition to retaining coaches Price and Chaney, Waldorf brought Wes Fry and Bob Tessier from NU, and he hired Hal Grant from USC as Cal's freshman coach.

Pappy emphasized to Grant that his primary job was to keep every player interested in football. Winning or losing games was of secondary importance. Hal would answer to Pappy only if a player turned in his uniform.

Another addition to Lynn's board of strategy was Edgar "Eggs" Manske, Cal's end coach. Eggs earned his nickname as a kid growing up in Nekoosa, Wisconsin, because he preferred sucking eggs to eating candy or drinking soda pop.

Manske earned a law degree from Chicago's Loyola University while playing pro ball. He had movie-star looks that captivated juries, but football was in his blood and he had gotten into coaching. The same approach that led to victory in a court of law also became the bedrock of his coaching and scouting philosophies: "Come to conclusions only after seeing things for yourself, always do your homework and don't waste time."

After Manske was hired, Pappy, Wes, Bob Tessier and Eggs had to go to Berkeley to conduct spring practice, and time was short, so they formed a four-man driving team and powered two cars straight through to the coast, taking turns at the wheel.

The long trip allowed plenty of time for Manske to be schooled in Waldorf's version of the T-Formation. Wes Fry told Manske that Waldorf's version of the "T" was built upon the shoulder block. Since most of Cal's returning offensive talent consisted of running backs, the Bears' attack would have to be run-oriented. Anyone who wanted to play end must, first and foremost, be a good blocker.

Eggs' initial contributions became teaching his ends how to block, strip interference and rush passers. He also became the Bears "super scout," and each year, the only Cal game Manske saw in person was the Big Game finale with Stanford.

Eggs always told his troops: "Next to quarterbacks, ends should be the smartest men on the team, because they're moving all around the field on every play and have to make correct decisions in split seconds."

Buoyed by literally hundreds of players - battle-toughened service veterans and talented kids from the rapidly growing state - Waldorf and his coaching staff merely had to sort the wheat from the chaff.

A legion of 255 candidates turned out for Cal's 1947 spring practice — some of whom had never even seen a football before.

"It was rough on us," said team manager Sedge Thompson, "but Pappy wanted an enthusiastic atmosphere. One kid lined up as a quarterback under a tackle. Pappy just looked at him and said, 'That cow's dry, son. Move over.' Then the kid lined up under the guard and Pappy said, 'That one's also dry. Keep movin' over.' He didn't show any sign of being mad or disgusted that entire spring."

Waldorf and his staff faced the extremely difficult task of selling themselves and their philosophy to a group of demoralized players they hadn't recruited or even seen play. Nearly all were from California.

Aside from Syracuse's trip to play USC when Waldorf was a player, and his attendance at the 1937 East-West Shrine Game, Waldorf had not been in the state before he was hired.

Some players were disappointed that Waldorf was their new coach because his won-loss record wasn't as impressive as Fritz Crisler's. So the coaches had to prove they could produce wins for Cal before they would gain the players' trust.

The coaching staff accomplished this goal through a masterful job of organization.

On the first day of spring practice, the players were handed copies of a detailed practice schedule. When they arrived in the locker room, they also saw it written on a blackboard. This schedule was followed to the letter.

Also, Waldorf took pride in knowing every player's first and last name. Even with hundreds of players trying out for the team, it wasn't difficult for Pappy to memorize players' names; he had mastered the technique years before. Waldorf associated each name with a mental image of the player's face or an unusual characteristic.

The morning sessions began with a one-hour "chalk talk" session, in which each assignment on every play was explained, along with how and why it was done.

For instance, Cal's running backs were instructed to line up in a three-point stance, because players might rock back in a two-point stance and could be flagged for a false start penalty. Each player was given a steno pad. The new head coach required they take notes and keep their notebooks neat and complete. They were also instructed to be prepared, that any staff member might ask to see the book without warning. This policy was enacted because Pappy knew the practice of "seeing it, reading it, then writing it" enhanced concentration.

This exercise also helped the players develop the life skills of thinking clearly, concisely and creatively.

There was no separation of players into offensive and defensive squads, because each player's position had not yet been determined. During drills, individual teaching was stressed and continued until assignments to the varsity and Rambler squads were announced.

Both players and assistant coaches acted quickly and efficiently. Everyone was constantly moving. There was no dead time. Regardless of whether or not the players had mastered the assigned chore, they turned to the next drill when the allotted time was up.

Pappy believed that snappy organization and drills run like clockwork were critical to morale and that lulls in activity led to unnecessarily long practices. He didn't want players to get bored and lose their competitive edge — and he especially didn't want precious time stolen from his players' studies.

Waldorf used three playing fields to scrimmage seven teams simultaneously. The list of drills for each group also contained the order of the players doing the drills. Pappy referred to these lists during practice to avoid wasting time scanning the landscape while keeping an eye on certain players.

The players soon discovered that no detail would be overlooked and absolutely nothing was taken for granted. They were taught, for example, that their huddles were to be formed the same distance from the line of scrimmage on each play and with players in their assigned positions. Thus, their opponents wouldn't be given any clue as to the play being called.

To discourage eavesdropping by opponents, the quarterback stood between the left end and left halfback and would speak only loudly enough for the left halfback to hear.

This tightly orchestrated program required a tremendous amount of work on the part of Pappy, his six full-time assistants and seven part-time student coaches. They each spent 2 1/2 hours preparing for each hour of practice.

By the time fall drills rolled around, Pappy immediately began establishing chummy relations with Bay Area sports writers. His theory was to disarm his critics in advance by making friends with them.

"Pappy taught me a lot about dealing with writers," said Paul Christopulos, Waldorf's closest confidant on the staff. "He always returned their phone calls, was truthful in his answers and made his comments general after he'd told the writers what they wanted to know. He was great copy and basically did the sports scribes' work for them."

Waldorf spent a good deal of time with the writers in the off season. With his big hello, high-elbow handshake, story-telling, limerick-reciting and infectious guffawing, he made fast friends with the men of the press.

At first, though, Pappy's hiring didn't impress the *San*

Francisco Examiner's Prescott Sullivan, who wrote: "Big, meaty Lynn O. 'Pappy' Waldorf is the new coach at the University of California. We realize there's nothing particularly distinctive about that. California's always getting a new football coach. Waldorf is the fourth the school has had in as many years. We hope Waldorf is a man of independent means. The job over there in Berkeley ain't too steady."

When Sullivan first visited the Cal head coach, he found Pappy to be pleasant, funny and very candid. Sullivan left with a smile on his face and a lot of quips and quotes in his notebook. He could easily write about the new coach in Berkeley. Sullivan considered how to best characterize Waldorf.

Prescott decided the man from Syracuse who had migrated to the Golden State should be called the "Walrus." After all, walruses are gregarious mammals who weigh a ton and can flourish on either the east or west coasts of North America, just like the beefy coach in Berkeley. So Sullivan began referring to Cal's coach as the "Walrus" in his newspaper columns, which is how Pappy acquired yet another nickname.

The first game of Waldorf's Cal career took place September 20, 1947, against Santa Clara in Memorial Stadium, before 45,000 curious fans.

Waldorf called the Bears' effort "ragged, but right," and California won, 33-7.

After the game, a huffing-and-puffing 285-pound Pappy made the first of many ascensions from the base of Strawberry Canyon to the locker room. He scaled 50 steep steps from the field through the stands and to the dressing room.

When Pappy arrived to address the press, huge beads of perspiration rolled from his brow, but he was beaming from ear to ear. Waldorf caught his breath and said, "I'm very happy and I think the kids are, too. We needed this first one and we got it."

Then, Pappy was interrupted by a loud chant from a crowd that had gathered outside: "We want Pappy! We want Pappy!"

A chorus of thousands of rooters implored Waldorf to speak to them from the dressing quarters' balcony. "Old Blue" Don Blessing explained to him that, on occasion, previous Cal coaches had made balcony speeches.

Pappy agreed, but not until game captain Rod Franz joined him.

"I've seen many schools play football, but never have I seen such spirit as at California," Pappy said in his first balcony speech. "I'm coaching a grand bunch of kids and we're darn proud of them. We made mistakes and we'll have to correct them before we play Navy. Now, I want to introduce our game captain, Rod Franz."

When Rod took the mike, he said simply, "We're gonna try to do the same damn thing to Navy next week."

At noon the following day came the debut of the "Second Guessers" show over Oakland's radio station KLX. *Oakland Tribune* sports editor Ed Schoenfeld collaborated with Waldorf for a half hour of conversation regarding the previous day's game and the Bears' prospects against their upcoming opponent.

When Schoenfeld proposed the show, he told the coach, "Don't worry, Lynn. I know we're not radio types. We'll just go on the air, a coach and a sports writer, and do the best we can. No strain."

Unfortunately, their best was not very good, but the show was so enticing in its quirky way that church officials claimed it affected their attendance.

Pappy had a deep, booming baritone and Schoenfeld had a squeaky, scratchy voice. But they were a riot.

Cal fans, meanwhile, looked forward to reading the Sunday paper for a change, thinking the headline would read, "It's a New Deal at Cal!" or "The Bears Are Back!

But they were wrong. Instead, they read large bold print screaming, "Fleet's In - Look Out Bears!" The paper pointed out the following week the culmination of "Operation Bear," a joint undertaking of the U.S. Naval Academy and Admiral Louis Denfield's First Task Fleet.

The Midshipmen had spent three weeks preparing for their game with Cal. The game was a centerpiece for a reunion of Admiral William Halsey's First Task Force.

It was, unquestionably, the biggest game in that part of the country and the Naval Academy's first game on the West Coast in 23 years. More than 20,000 Naval personnel of every rank would be cheering for the Middies.

A throng of 83,000 fans overflowed Memorial Stadium, a record for that arena, and they saw the Bears build a 14-0 lead, thanks to Bob Celeri's rushing TD and another score set up by Waldorf.

From his 34-yard line, Jackie Jensen hit left guard for three, then Celeri intentionally threw an incomplete pass. The

Middies expected another pass and deployed their defense accordingly. Celeri dropped back, faked a throw and then handed off to Jensen on a draw play.

Jackie shot through a wide hole at right guard, stepped over a fallen defender and trotted 63 yards for a score without a hand laid on him.

In the closing two minutes of action, Navy blocked Jensen's punt, recovered the ball at Cal's 2-yard line and scored to make it 14-7.

The Midshipmen beautifully executed an onside kick, but their final threat ended with Jensen's interception.

After that huge Bear victory, the scene outside Memorial Stadium was almost the same as the previous week, with 15,000 rooters gathered beneath the balcony, shouting, "We want Pappy! We want Pappy!"

Pappy appeared, then said, "I'm doggone happy. I just want to say for all my boys and coaches that we're real proud of what happened. Our boys played a real tough ball game, kept the pressure on and I'm proud of them. Now, I want to introduce the most improved player on our squad, George Fong."

Fong, a hard running Chinese-American halfback from San Francisco, was caught off-guard by the introduction. After the game, he had stripped naked to relax. He had to hustle into a pair of football pants and a jersey so he could go out on the balcony to stammer a few words.

With three straight victories under their belts, the Bears' next assignment included a long rail trip to Madison, Wisconsin, for a test against the University of Wisconsin on October 11th.

Chapter 4

Before the game, Waldorf tried to help relieve his players' anxiety by confessing, "Nervous? I'm not at all nervous. As you can see, I'm wearing the coat from one suit and the trousers from another."

Pappy shouldn't have worried. Cal blistered Wisconsin, 48-7, and he used all 37 players taken on the trip.

The Bears continued on their rampage, then faced Southern Cal, West Coast football's standard of excellence. They had a chance to prove how far they had come since 1946.

The Trojans were undefeated. In their previous four games, they held their opponents to a combined 288 yards on the ground, giving up only two touchdowns.

Four special trains brought 4,000 SC rooters to the game. Tickets were easily scalped for $25 each. Nationally known broadcaster Red Barber was in town to call the game coast-to-coast over CBS Radio.

In the locker room before the game, Waldorf showed his players how proud he was of their accomplishments. He asked them to decide among themselves what their first play from scrimmage would be. Following a brief discussion, they chose "18," a counter play in which right halfback Jack Swaner carried around left end.

The Bears blocked it to perfection and Swaner sailed 65 yards for a touchdown.

The first half was a fan's delight, showcasing two explosive offenses. USC was ahead 20-14 at the break, and that turned out to be Cal's high-water mark.

Cal's lack of experienced linebackers was exposed in the second half, and the Trojans won, 39-14.

A most unusual tribute occurred at the end of the game. Waldorf, the coach whose team had just lost by 25 points, was given a standing ovation by the Cal cheering sections. His team may have trailed on the scoreboard that day, but the rooters thanked him for bringing the Bears back from the depths of despair.

Pappy apologized to the fans during his balcony speech after that game, saying, "I'm sorry I failed you."

But they shouted back, "No, you didn't. What do you mean, you let us down? Look at last year!"

Pappy answered, "This gang is naturally feeling down. I want you to help bring them up. I can say to this team in defeat something perhaps I couldn't have said in victory - this is the finest group of young men I have ever been associated with."

The next day, when the "Second Guessers" radio show began, Pappy began with this announcement, "You know Ed, as I drove by the campus to come to the station, I noticed the campanile was still standing."

That year began a fantastic run, one of the most spectacular in Cal history. The Bears went 9-1, then ran off consecutive regular-season records of 10-0, 10-0 and 9-0-1.

As for 1948, Pappy's second season, there were so many key players returning, only a Rose Bowl bid would satisfy the Bears, because it would silence the doubters once and for all.

nn and Louise Waldorf, a couple who inspired friends, family and countless thousands for
ore than a half-century.

Rev. Ernest Waldorf, Lynn's father, was a famous speaker in addition to his duties as a Methodist bishop.

Lynn Waldorf, proud graduate of East High in Cleveland.

The college man: Lynn was dapper, popular and successful at Syracuse University in the early 1920s.

Lynn and Louise on their wedding day, 1925.

nn got a taste of big-time, cross-country football rivalries when his Syracuse team faced uthern California in Los Angeles in 1924.

ways willing to compete, Lynn *(third from left)* was a member of the Syracuse rowing ım.

The Waldorf family at home: Mary Louise, Pappy, Louise, Caroline.

Pappy was a great teacher in addition to being a famous football coach and took pride in his knowledge of things outside athletics.

A nickname takes root: Northwestern assistant coach Burt Ingwersen *(front right)* calle Lynn "Pappy" and the handle stuck for life. Pappy *(front left)* and Burt were joined on t 1940 fishing expedition by *(rear from left)* Tug Wilson, Iowa athletic director Dad Schro and resort owner Joe Parenteau.

The Waldorf family at home for Christmas, 1948. (l-r) Fannie McKay, Pappy, Louise, Carolyn (sitting) and Mary Louise (standing).

Pappy Waldorf's first Cal coaching staff, a group that everyone associated with those early Bear teams agrees was among the best in football: *(back from left)* Eggs Manske, Nibs Price, Hal Grant, Wes Fry; *(front from left)* Zeb Chaney, Waldorf, Bob Tessier.

Waldorf loved his teams to run the football, but he knew passing talent when he had it. Gunslinger Bob Celeri (22) shared duties as quarterback with Dick Erickson when Cal made it to the Rose Bowl following the 1948 season.

Pappy's post-game balcony speeches to fans outside Memorial Stadium became command performances.

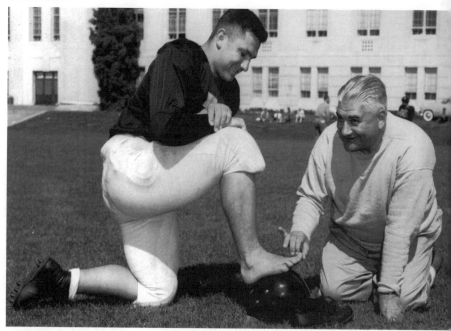

Jim *(Truck)* Cullom was one of Waldorf's favorite players and not just because Cullom was a fine lineman and outstanding kicker. Truck also possessed a quick wit that kept teammates loose and Pappy smiling.

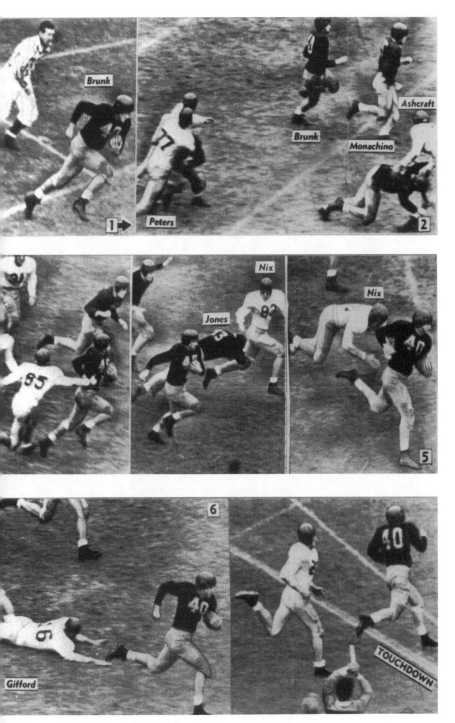

One of the most famous dashes in California history. With the Bears trailing USC 10-7 in the fourth quarter of their 1949 showdown, Frank Brunk ran back a kickoff 102 yards for a game-winning touchdown, leaving Trojan star Frank Gifford on his belly.

Cal gets a touchdown from Jack Swaner to help defeat Stanford in the 1949 Big Game.

Pappy greets well-wishers as the Bears arrive in Pasadena for the 1950 Rose Bowl against Ohio State.

repping for the '50 Rose Bowl: Pappy poses with *(from left)* All American Rod Franz, orrest Klein, Dan Begovich and Bob Celeri.

couple of big Bears: Pappy always enjoyed the lighter moments of football, which included lowning around with Cal's famous mascot, Oski.

Cal's Jim Monachino (35) leaps to snare a Bob Celeri pass against USC in 1950.

Safety and punt returner Carl Van Heuit wasn't particularly big or swift, but under the tutelage of Pappy and his assistants, Van Heuit became an All American at Cal.

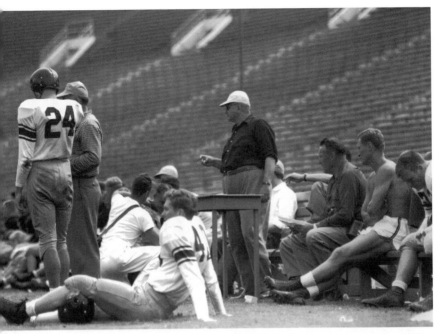

ways organized, always prepared, Pappy instructs the troops during spring practice, 1951.

appy with two of his greatest players, guard/linebacker Les Richter (67) and running back hnny Olszewski.

Pappy works the sidelines against Stanford in 1951. The Big Game between Cal and Stanford is a season-maker (or breaker) for both schools Pappy posted a 7-1-2 record against the Bears' Bay Area rival.

In addition to coaching, teaching and absorbing information on subjects as diverse at Shakespeare, the Civil War and bird-watching, Pappy was also an author, autographing copies of *This Game of Football*.

tline to come.

appy always had a special bond with Cal fans – especially the school band. On the night he announced his resignation in 1956, several band members made an impromptu hike to the Waldorf house for a special seranade.

Two of Pappy's former players, All American running back Jackie Jensen (left) and quarterback Boots Erb, became partners in a well-known Oakland restaurant, The Bow & Bell. The eatery opened in 1953, so '63 called for a 10th anniversary birthday cake.

Pappy's famous *Prayer for an Unbeliever* was read at a memorial serice after his death and has been quoted countless times. This is the original, written by Pappy on San Francisco 49ers stationary and sent to Jan Erickson, wife of former Cal quarterback Dick Erickson.

SAN FRANCISCO
FORTY NINERS
1255 POST STREET • SAN FRANCISCO, CALIFORNIA 94109 • PRospect 1-

Sepd. 1 —

Work in progress—
This is the 3 A.M. or "Bourbon" draft —

A prayer for an unbeliever

To whom it may concern—
From those who talk and seldom act —
From those who take and never give —
Deliver us
From over-kill and under-care
From lack of water and polluted air
Save us
To walk a ways in the other man's shoes
Lead us
For this small, stagnant pool from the
river of our dreams
Forgive us.

Well I tried anyhow —

Lynn O. Waldorf

The Waldorf clan gathered at a party to celebrate Pappy's retirement from the 49ers in 1972: *(front row from left)* Becky Osborne, Carolyn Pickering, Mary Louise Osborne; *(second row from left)* Bruce Osborne, Jerry Pickering II, Mike Pickering; *(back row from left)* Steve Osborne, Jerry Pickering, Louise Waldorf, Pappy Waldorf, Bunt Osborne.

One of the greatest tributes to Lynn Waldorf - coach and gentleman - is the existence of Pappy's Boys, a group of former Cal players, staff and special friends who still meet and work to keep Pappy's legacy alive. Pappy's Boys managed to get funding and university approval for a statue of the legendary coach, which sits in Faculty Glade at the University of California. Among those present at the dedication ceremonies were *(from left)* Ray Willsey, Dick Erickson, Jim Cullom, Dr. John Najarian, Rod Franz and Pete Schabarum.

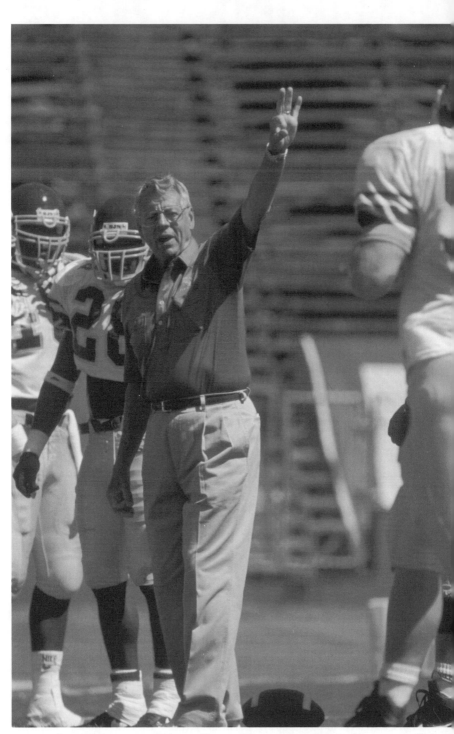

Dozens of Pappy's former pupils have gone on to forge spectacular coaching careers of their own, including John Ralston, two-time Rose Bowl winner and later a NFL coach. Ralston has said that he patterned his career – and his life – after Pappy Waldorf. He finished his coaching career at San José State (above) where he remains on staff as an advisor.

Going 9-1 in '47, though, was no guarantee of success in 1948. The coaches stressed that each player would need an extra boost to achieve that level of play that could make them champions.

The Bears got what they needed when fall practice began. As running back Charley Sarver described it, "We were in the training room getting taped, when all of a sudden, we heard a loud 'Wham!' It sounded like an explosion. It was Rod Franz hitting a blocking dummy. But there was still a good 30 minutes before practice was to begin.

"This continued for four days. Then, on the fifth day, two guys joined Rod doing all this extra blocking work and everybody else started doing extra drills. Pretty soon, the coaches started showing up early.

"Even though practice was scheduled to begin at 2:30, pre-practice started 30 minutes before.

"Also, (tackle) Jim Cullom started a chant: 'Ten rivers to cross!' Everybody picked it up, and during drills, running backs would take a handoff, then run all the way to the end zone. Not only that, their blockers would make their block, get up, then run all the way downfield after the backs.

"Meanwhile, everyone's chanting, 'Ten rivers to cross!' After each win, we'd count it down: 'Nine more rivers to cross,' 'Eight more rivers to cross,' et cetera."

The key to the Bears' success was their offensive line, which was had been molded by the gifted Tessier. He told his players at Berkeley, just as he had at Northwestern, "You're not really hurt until your shoes are filled with blood."

The right guard had the toughest job of any lineman, and All-American Rod Franz filled the bill. Nobody was better at stepping around Cal's right tackle and taking out the left linebacker.

Waldorf said of him, "At first, I thought Rod was the best defensive guard I'd seen since Ohio State's Warren Amling in 1945, but later, I realized he was the hardest charging defensive guard I'd seen in 23 years of coaching."

Franz' teammate, Frank "Bud" Van Deren, said, "He's the only man who went full speed, even between plays."

Franz' play was so exceptional, he became California's only three-time All-American.

Next to Rod Franz, Truck Cullom — a 5-foot-11, 224-pound sophomore, was Cal's best lineman. Though he had never even seen a rugby game, Cullom went out for Cal's rugby squad, and became a great player.

During a practice session, Cal's legendary rugby coach, Doc Hudson, noticed Cullom's prodigious gut and said, "You, the truck. Come here and line up as a prop."

Cullom was an imperturbable, always-wisecracking left tackle who was also an exceptional placekicker. He was as quick off the line as he was with a quip and was a master at downfield blocking.

Jim's tremendous sense of humor helped his teammates and coaches deal with the pressures of such high ambitions. When Waldorf opened one team meeting by saying, "You are the finest group of young men I've ever been privileged to coach,"

Truck interjected, "You're a pretty good group yourself, Pappy."

By 1948, Jackie Jensen, at 5-foot-11 and 195 pounds, had become the team's best overall football player, as well as its best fullback. During that season, he carried the ball 137 times for 1,010 yards and six touchdowns - Cal's first 1,000-yard rusher in history. Jackie was chosen as fullback on seven of the nine major All-American lists in 1948.

Of Jensen's almost magical running style, Pappy once said: "He eludes the hand he cannot see."

Cal had two very good, but very different quarterbacks in Dick Erickson and Bob Celeri.

Erickson, nicknamed "Old Faithful" or "Money in the Bank" by the local writers, started most games because he was ice-cube cool under pressure and was unlikely to fumble snaps. Fumbles were common in the late 1940s when college teams began using the T-Formation.

Waldorf was deathly afraid of fumbles during the early stages of a game when players are most tense. Cal's coaches had supreme confidence in Erickson and believed he was the most underrated quarterback on the coast. And less susceptible to mistakes.

Erickson tended to be conservative in his play calling, due to the multitude of outstanding running backs who took his handoffs. Celeri, on the other hand, was anything but conservative. With his skinny legs, snake hips, large hands and unusually long fingers, he possessed great foot speed and loved to fake handoffs, put the ball on his hip, roll out, then fire a deep pass or take off running.

The 1948 season was the first during which the Bears flew on road trips, which presented a difficulty for Pappy.

"When it became evident that Cal's road trip to play Navy would be by plane," manager Sedge Thompson said, "Pappy's fear of flying became known. An unfortunate experience riding an old Jenny in Oklahoma City nearly 25 years before was an experience he just couldn't put behind him.

"During a meeting that week, somebody said, 'Oh, Pappy, when your number's up, your number's up.' Pappy replied, 'That's all right for you, but what if the pilot's number's up?'

"When we got on the plane, Pappy sat in an aisle seat so he wouldn't be near a window and see anything that would frighten him more. As we passed over Arizona, the pilot thought he'd give us a treat by circling over the Grand Canyon. Pappy stared straight ahead, knuckles white from gripping the armrests. Somebody said, 'Wow! Isn't that great!'

"All Pappy said was, 'Some ditch.' "

The 1948 season was truly historic for Cal football - a new single-season scoring record, a new attendance mark and an unbeaten regular season.

The Golden Bears expected to go to the Rose Bowl. However, in the unpredictable world of college football, winning them all didn't necessarily mean a ticket to Pasadena — at least not then.

Chapter 5

THE MARK OF CAIN

The subject is open to debate, of course, but you might easily make the argument that the 1949 Rose Bowl was the most bizarre "great game" in football history.

For starters, merely determining the participants followed a convoluted path.

In those days, college football was one of America's sports passions and the largest-ever lineup of bowl games was played following the 1948 season. Achieving an unbeaten season, however, did not guarantee a bowl bid that year, as the University of California found out.

Going back to the 1947 Rose Bowl, the game had become a matchup of a Pacific Coast Conference team against a Big Ten opponent. Skeptics reminded anyone who would listen that the Big Ten was really the "Big Nine" because the University of Chicago had abandoned its athletic department and no replacement had yet come on board. They also sneered at the "three-year, no-repeat" provision for Big Ten squads.

This meant that in 1948, the Big Ten's entry in the 1949 Rose Bowl was Northwestern, which was the conference's runner-up with a 7-2 record.

Meanwhile, California had gone 10-0, with a 6-0 mark in the conference. However, a problem surfaced in determining the PCC champion because the Bears weren't scheduled to play the University of Oregon, and the '48 Ducks were one of that school's best teams ever.

Oregon's conference record that year was 7-0, better than Cal's, but the Ducks were 9-1 overall. They'd lost a September road game to Michigan, the 1948 national champion, 14-0. Strangely, that loss attracted more national acclaim for Oregon than California could muster with its unbeaten season.

After playing Oregon, Michigan coach Fritz Crisler proclaimed Duck quarterback Norm Van Brocklin, "... the finest passer I've ever seen."

Sports writers likewise became enthralled by the exploits of Van Brocklin, "The Arm of Oregon," and California's narrow win over Stanford added fuel to the argument that Oregon was the only West Coast team capable of beating any Big Ten participant in the Rose Bowl, even runner-up Northwestern.

Oregon and Cal were declared PCC co-champions, but the Rose Bowl bid was decided by ballots telegraphed to Commissioner Vic Schmidt in Los Angeles. Since 10 votes were cast, a possibility existed for a tie.

In that event, Oregon would go to the Rose Bowl, since — of the two schools — California had made the most recent appearance in Pasadena.

At that time, the Pacific Coast Conference had, in effect, two divisions - the "Big Money Division" consisting of the four California members plus Washington, and the "Pacific Northwest Poor Farms," — the two Oregon schools, Washington State, Montana and Idaho. None of the big money schools were expected to vote for Oregon, so the best the Ducks could hope for was that the schools with smaller stadiums and revenues would force a tie.

The thought of a tie was frightening to the Tournament of Roses Committee, because they couldn't envision Oregon being a strong enough attraction to generate a Rose Bowl sellout.

Pappy Waldorf, meanwhile, had been on an emotional roller coaster all that fateful Monday morning. One moment it seemed he could assume his Bears would cross that last river to the Rose Bowl, but the next instant, uncertainty brought a sinking feeling to the pit of his stomach.

As the morning dragged on, Pappy realized he wouldn't know the Rose Bowl decision by the time he left the UC campus for a speaking engagement at The Family, a men's club in San Francisco.

Waldorf had built his coaching career on trusting his players and assistant coaches; now the time had come for him to trust in the fairness of those who voted on the PCC's Rose Bowl representative. After 23 years of college coaching, he felt experienced at handling events he had no control over, but this was destined to be a day on which he truly would learn the anguish of uncertainty.

Pappy's trip to San Francisco included a seven-mile drive across the Bay Bridge. Midday traffic was light and Waldorf was alone with his thoughts. He nervously puffed on a cigar until the noon newscast began. Pappy leaned over to turn on a brand-new radio that had just been installed in his Pontiac, but all he heard was silence. His fingers frantically twisted the radio's knobs, to no avail. In desperation, he slammed the heel of his hand against the radio, but still nothing happened.

Waldorf was so flustered, he didn't notice that he had broken his cigar. He realized however he was going to miss learning firsthand the results of the biggest vote he had ever faced. The decision would be announced while he was on a long drive across a lonely bridge.

Pappy's shock turned to disgust. Why wouldn't his brand-new radio work? There had to be a loose connection, a malfunction of some sort, but he couldn't stop the car in the middle of the bridge to fiddle with it. He knew he would learn the outcome of the voting when he arrived at The Family, because the looks on the faces of his friends would tell the tale.

Waldorf decided that the solitude was intended to prepare him for learning the outcome, because at this point, his team's future actions were carried on the capricious wings of others' judgment. Pappy used the time to ponder the situation and to find words that might help these young men deal with the frustration of an undefeated season falling short of a Rose Bowl bid, should that occur.

Cal's players ought to be proud of putting forth their best effort to bring respect to the university and to the Golden Bears, regardless of which way the voting went, he thought. Pappy would remind them that only two years before, California football wasn't taken seriously. He would tell them how thrilling it had been for him to watch the players, young men of various backgrounds and personalities, learn to respect and trust each other. They had learned lessons they could carry with them throughout their lives.

Playing in a Rose Bowl would have been a bonus, but it was a postseason event, not the reason for playing football. However, it was difficult to focus on that fact, because if anyone deserved to go to the Rose Bowl, his boys did.

The drive seemed endless. When Pappy arrived at the club, he strode in briskly, but quickly noticed the lobby was empty. He was reminded that the rest of the world was going on without a thought of the Rose Bowl.

Judging by the lack of familiar faces of San Francisco sports writers, Pappy surmised they had apparently staked out the UC campus. He walked over to the main desk, but before he could ask for a phone, he was given a message to call Greg Engelhard, Cal's assistant athletic director.

Pappy's thick index finger whirled the phone's dialer and when Engelhard answered, all Waldorf heard was: "We're in."

The weight of the world was lifted from Pappy's shoulders. Just then, a group of writers showed up and saw Pappy's eyes twinkling, with a smile bigger than they'd ever seen on the coach who was always happy.

"I'm going to buy a new fedora for Chet Gargas," Waldorf said. "When I took this job, he bet me a new hat that Cal would be in the Rose Bowl in two years. Chet played on my 1936 Big Ten Champion team and is now Northwestern's assistant athletic director.

"I'm telling you this because I want you to know what I'm going up against when I face Northwestern. They remember me, they believe in me, but on New Year's Day, nothing would please them more than to thrash their old coach."

The California-Northwestern matchup produced a great human interest story - the teacher, Pappy Waldorf against the pupil, NU coach Bob Voigts.

Voigts and most of his assistants had played for Waldorf, and it was Lynn's recommendation that resulted in Voigts getting his first head coaching job.

Cal had the deeper team, because Northwestern had a starting 15, substituting only four players when the Cats went on defense. Pappy had also coached or recruited nearly all of the Wildcats during his years in Evanston. The advantages of depth and the intimate knowledge Cal had about Northwestern's players, though, was offset somewhat by NU having more experienced players.

Another factor was the overall importance of the game. To Cal, as with all West Coast teams, the goal was to make an appearance at the Rose Bowl.

However, for Northwestern's players, playing in the Rose Bowl would signify the game of their lives, because the Big Ten's three-year, no-repeat provision, in effect, stipulated 1949 would be the only time this particular group of players would be eligible for a Pasadena appearance.

Voigts shrewdly managed the situation after Northwestern arrived in southern California. He refused to return a "Key to the City of Pasadena" so that everyone would understand that the Cats intended to take a lot more than the key. Then he barred West Coast writers from NU's practices to eliminate distractions. When the local press heaped abuse on the Wildcats, he used those newspaper clippings to fire up his players.

Voigts also ran a tight ship. He cloistered his team in Pasadena's Huntington Hotel and scheduled a practice on Christmas Eve.

However, he wasn't Ebenezer Scrooge. After the players dressed, they were told, "All right, everybody sing some Christmas carols." Then they were dismissed.

Pappy, on the other hand, was determined to see that his boys didn't miss Christmas with their families. He gave the team two days off, and Cal didn't head south to their Rose Bowl headquarters at Riverside's Mission Inn until a week before the game.

Rain poured all day December 27 in Riverside when Cal resumed Rose Bowl workouts, and the dark clouds were an omen of misfortune for the Golden Bears. During a drill, Pete Schabarum jumped up with Jackie Jensen, trying to knock down a pass.

When he came down, Pete's cleated football shoe landed on Jensen's right foot, rupturing blood vessels in Jackie's big toe. This injury was especially worrisome, since Jack was the team's best punter as well as their best ballcarrier. A special steel plate was inserted in Jensen's right shoe to protect his painful toe.

Even happy-go-lucky, always-ready-with-a-quip Truck Cullom was having a bad time in Riverside. Truck had arranged to be married January 2, but when his fiancee, Martha Jordan, arrived in Los Angeles on December 29, she was diagnosed with chicken pox.

Luckily for Jim, Cal's schedule of practices had prevented him from meeting her, because if he had, he would have been quarantined along with others to whom his bride-to-be had been exposed. Martha was originally ordered to postpone the wedding, but Jim and Martha managed to obtain a dispensation from the local board of health and the wedding took place as scheduled.

Since both Northwestern and Cal had strong running attacks, and NU led the nation in pass defense, the game figured to be an orgy of brawn. NU had little depth, with only 25 players available for a tight game. It was questionable if the thin Wildcat squad could hold up to an afternoon of pounding.

Cal's coaches figured they were capable of scoring more points than Northwestern, because NU didn't have any players the caliber of Jensen. The majority of their practice time focused on using plays in the first half that would set up "counters" and "misdirections" in the second half.

As far as Cal's defense was concerned, the Wildcats lacked a passing threat because their quarterback, Don Burson, was suffering from an inflammation of his arm muscles so severe that he could barely grip a football. Cal's scouts informed Pappy of this, but he was wary — no one can predict the extent to which a player's injury will affect his performance during a game.

So there were two huge question marks - Don Burson's right arm and Jackie Jensen's right big toe.

Dick LemMon and Carl Van Heuit were two Ramblers traveling with the Cal team to Riverside. LemMon's assignment was to imitate Ed Tunnicliff running NU's "Direct Snap" play. Litz Rusness, who was still scouting for Pappy after 13 years, advised Waldorf that with Burson's arm problems, the deceptive, wide-running "Direct Snap" was the only tactic Northwestern could use to score quickly. Still, it was Rusness' opinion that the Wildcats would have to be within their opponent's 20-yard line before they could attempt it.

Van Heuit's role was to imitate Frank Aschenbrenner, the Northwestern back the Bears feared most. Since Rusness warned Cal's coaches of Aschenbrenner's upper body strength, the first defender to hit Van Heuit was instructed to grab him around the waist, then hold him until others arrived to swarm tackle. Carl took a brutal beating that week, but never complained.

Pappy rewarded LemMon and Van Heuit for their contributions by suiting them up for the big show. At first, Dick LemMon had mixed feelings, because if he was sent into the game, he would lose a year of eligibility. However, later he discovered the thrill of being on the sidelines during a Rose Bowl game.

Years later, Carl Van Heuit shared a special memory of that Rose Bowl: "After the final pregame practice session was over, three of my friends from Berkeley approached me to say hello and to ask if any tickets were available for the game. I told them Coach Waldorf might have some, but I was very reluctant to ask him. They prevailed upon me, so I talked with Pappy. He gave one of his deep chuckles, reached into his pocket and pulled out some game tickets. He asked me how many I needed and when I said 'Three,' he said, 'Here's four. Another friend may show up before game time.' "

New Year's Day, 1949, the temperature was a clammy 50 degrees and the sky was overcast, threatening rain. When the teams took the field, they discovered the stadium's surface was sandy and rock-hard with no sign of grass, just rye grass seedling frustrated from unusually heavy December rains. In desperation, the Rose Bowl's dirt had been painted green.

And finally, it was time to play.

Neither team could gain a first down on their initial possessions. Then, suddenly, Frank Aschenbrenner carried off right tackle, spun out of Will Lotter's grasp and ran 73 yards for a touchdown - a Rose Bowl record. Northwestern was ahead, 7-0.

After the ensuing kickoff, Cal had the ball on their 33-yard line. Erickson had called a fullback slant to the left with a blocking scheme that gave Jensen the choice of cutting off tackle or around end. On the snap, Truck Cullom pulled out of the line and led interference against the right side of the NU defense.

Jensen flew past Northwestern tackle Steve Sawle's reach, Van Deren slammed Murakowski out of the way and Cunningham blocked Tom Worthington out of the runner's path.

Just as suddenly as Aschenbrenner had shocked the Bears, the favor was returned. Jensen dashed 67 yards to tie the game 7-7.

After those two long touchdown runs in the game's first eight and a half minutes, the contest bogged down into a defensive struggle with a lot of hard hitting, but no points.

Midway through the second quarter, however, the Wildcats pulled off a play which proved Voigts and his assistants had done their homework.

Before Jensen dropped back to punt, he noticed Johnny Miller was in to receive the kick. Waldorf's scouts had cautioned Cal's coaches Miller had incredible acceleration and could go all the way, anytime.

Jensen was unconcerned, though. He knew he would punt the ball so high it would either sail out of bounds or that Cal's punt coverage would have time to swarm downfield, swallowing up anyone who attempted a return.

So Jackie launched the punt. The ball gained altitude, peaked, then floated downward into Miller's arms at Northwestern's 38-yard line. Miller began running to his right, gave ground, then, shockingly, handed the ball to Tom Worthington, who had peeled back after originally being deployed as a blocker for the return.

Worthington took off along the sideline, heading for the end zone. This reverse completely surprised California. Only Jensen's saving tackle at Cal's 22-yard line prevented a touchdown.

The Wildcats pounded away on the ground, and Murakowski gave Northwestern a first down less than a yard from the goal line with a take-no-prisoners, fourth-down run.

There's was no doubt that Murakowski would get the call again from there, but when he did, Cal end Norm Pressley rushed in from the outside.

The rules stated the ball had to break the plane of the goal line for a play to be ruled a touchdown. Pressley grabbed both of Archie's arms from behind, hoping to cause a fumble.

And in a flash, the ball came free.

Cal's Will Lotter fell on it in the end zone. But was it a fumble, or had Murakowski broken the plane of the goal line before the ball was pulled loose.

The crowd looked to referee Jimmy Cain for the decision. In those days, only a referee could officially signal the call.

Field judge Jay Berwanger, a legendary player in his own right, had straddled the goal line as the play unfolded.

Berwanger emphatically pointed at the goal stripe to indicate that Murakowski had scored. Since Berwanger was in perfect position and was so emphatic in his gestures, Cain signaled a touchdown for Northwestern.

There was little discussion at the time in the pressbox. Only the *Los Angeles Times'* Braven Dyer said it wasn't a touchdown.

Meanwhile, the blocking broke down on Northwestern's PAT attempt, causing Jim Farrar's kick to sail wide. The Wildcats had taken the lead, 13-7, and that remained the score when the teams went to the dressing room at the half.

When play resumed, Cal confidently went to its long-planned counter action, plays set up by Jensen's runs in the first half.

And then...disaster.

Jensen rolled out to the right and had the choice of running with the ball or throwing downfield. Northwestern's defense dropped and Jensen appeared to have a clear track ahead to the end zone, when he suddenly collapsed without a hand laid on him.

As it turned out, a tender hamstring Jack had nursed that season gave out at the worst possible time. Jensen was carried off the field and the Bears' hopes were crippled by the loss of the player upon whom their offense was built.

Cal's coaching staff had planned to use Schabarum as Jensen's replacement, but Jackie suggested that Waldorf put in the coolest man under pressure he knew - his roommate, Frank Brunk.

Waldorf waved Brunk over and told him to go in at fullback. When Frank entered Cal's huddle, Truck Cullom said, "Brunk's in at fullback. Look's like we'll have to start blocking."

With Paul Keckley and Staten Webster doing some work, Cal marched downfield, but ground to a halt at the NU 4. On fourth and goal, Cal had come too far to settle for a field goal.

Erickson handed off to Jack Swaner, who ran through Pee Wee Day's high tackling attempt and barreled into the end zone. Cullom's PAT kick was good and California led, 14-13, with 1:39 remaining in the third quarter.

The fourth period opened with California in possession of the ball, first and 10 at Northwestern's 43. Nine plays later, it was fourth and goal at Northwestern's 5-yard line and, against their usual tendencies, Cal's coaches decided to throw.

At the snap, John Cunningham blasted off the line of scrimmage, ran toward the right corner of the end zone, then cut toward the goal post. He was on his tip-toes in the end zone, with his 6-foot-4 frame stretched to its full length as he reached for the pass flying toward him, but the ball glanced off his fingertips.

Northwestern was still alive.

But Cal wouldn't budge, and with the fourth quarter winding down, the Bears punted Northwestern inside its own 10-yard line.

On first down, Tunnicliff carried the ball off left tackle, but was cartwheeeled by Stormy Hileman after only a yard gain. Tunnicliff landed on the back of his neck after pinwheeling through the air, and the ball rolled out of his arms.

George Souza pounced on the fumble and claimed possession for Cal. With less than five minutes left in the game, Souza's recovery at Northwestern's 13 had evidently locked up a Rose Bowl triumph for the Golden Bears.

Except that Jimmy Cain ruled there was no fumble!

Referee Cain maintained he had blown his whistle before the football had rolled out of Tunnicliff's arms to " ... prevent Tunnicliff from serious injury."

Northwestern got new life from Cain's quick whistle but time was running out. Burson handed off to Aschenbrenner, who swept to the right, then instead of slashing and battering his way for yards, Frank pulled up and fired a pass to Don Stonesifer, who leaped, snatched the ball and fell to the turf at the NU 30.

Since Art Murakowski was out of the game with injured ribs, Gaspar Perricone, the Cats' hard-nosed fullback, got the call. He took Burson's handoff, patted down his leather helmet with his free hand to ready himself for a collision, unloaded on Frank Van Deren and plodded 15 yards to NU's 45.

Aschenbrenner then took a pitchout and tried to cut through the right side, but Tim Minahen held him to a 2-yard gain. Tunnicliff carried over left guard to the 50, which would have been a difficult third and five, but a penalty flag had been thrown.

With four minutes left in the game, Bud Van Deren had played his heart out and was dead on his feet. As he was leaving the field for a brief rest, Sarkisian cunningly snapped the ball on a quick count. Cal was penalized for having 12 men on the field.

Suddenly, Northwestern had a very attainable second and three situation at Cal's 48. It took two plays and some brutal work from Perricone, but the Cats got their first down at the Bear 45 as rain began to fall, turning the bare field into a sea of mud.

Just slightly more than three minutes remained. Northwestern trailed by a point and Art Murakowski, one of their best running backs, was injured and out of the game. Their quarterback's passing arm was useless. Even if the Wildcats managed to move the ball close enough to try a long field goal, no one on the team was capable of such a kick. They could only win if they could score a touchdown.

Frank Aschenbrenner swept to the right on first down, looked as if he was pulling up to throw another pass, tried an end run, but was horse-collared by Celeri after only a two-yard gain. It was second and eight from Cal's 43-yard line.

Litz Rusness' scouting reports had told Pappy and his assistants that NU wouldn't try anything but off-tackle runs outside their opponent's 20-yard line.

But Voigts decided to go against his tendency.

Burson broke the Wildcats out of their huddle and, as they lined up, was practically unnoticed when he positioned himself behind Sarkisian, but slightly to Sarkie's left. Tunnicliff went in motion from left to right, apparently to flare downfield and get open for a pass.

As Tunnicliff passed behind Burson, Sarkisian snapped the ball. Burson rose out of his crouch, allowing the ball to pass by his right leg, but Tunnicliff actually received the snap. Burson continued to execute a fake lateral to Aschenbrenner as a deception.

The fake created a moment of confusion, allowing Tunnicliff to get downfield. Northwestern had never used the play outside the 20-yard line and Burson's Academy Award performance with his fake lateral sucked in Cal's left defensive end.

NU guard Ed Nemeth sealed off most of California's pursuit. Minahen and Celeri raced across the field looking for an angle on Tunnicliff, but Wildcat tackle Bill Forman flew through the air and landed belly to the ground creating an obstacle that kept the Cal players from catching Tunnicliff.

As Tunnicliff approached the end zone, a defender came zooming toward him. It was Brunk, the forgotten man who had fearlessly filled in for Jensen.

Brunk was the last hope of saving the game for California. He flew all the way across the field, but was a heartbeat too late. Brunk made contact, but slid off Tunnicliff's back and Northwestern had its miracle touchdown.

Jim Farrar's PAT kick was good and Northwestern led, 20-14, with 1:59 left.

The Bears began their last possession on their own 21, and made things exciting when Swaner gained 17 yards and Celeri found Brunk with a pass for 17 more.

With the ball at NU's 45, Celeri tried again, but he was sacked for an 11-yard loss.

Fifty-five seconds remained and the Golden Bears were 56 yards from victory. Celeri elected to throw to Charley Sarver, the "Bakersfield Bullet."

Years later, Sarver recalled that moment: "My favorite play was when I was flanked right, then ran a streak route down the sideline. I'd get the defensive halfback going along at my speed, then I'd pour it on and slant to the inside. It had worked all year and would've worked at that moment.

"All season long, Celeri had thrown either long or right on the money. During that Rose Bowl, though, Celeri was short with his throws all day.

"Looking back, I wish I'd told Celeri, 'Rather than break to the goal post, I'm going to cut out.' But I didn't and the play ran right into that safety's area."

Celeri's throw was intercepted by Pee Wee Day, and Cal was beaten.

When the game ended moments later, the pupil and the teacher shook hands at midfield.

"You've got a nice team, Bob," Waldorf said.

Voights replied in kind.

Then Pappy said: "If I had to lose, I'm glad at least it was to one of my All-Americans."

There was no more time for any more words, as rain-drenched, jubilant Wildcats lifted Bob Voigts on their shoulders and carried him off the field.

After the Northwestern players had returned onto their locker room, happily exhausted from the tough ballgame, they slumped on benches, packing trunks and even the floor, trying to muster up the energy to put on their street clothes. A familiar visitor entered their dressing quarters. Pappy Waldorf had come to see them. There was quiet as he spoke.

"Today, I felt I couldn't lose," Pappy said. "You are all my boys."

For Cal, however, the 20-14 defeat was bitter almost beyond belief. To begin with, Pappy basically was facing a team he had recruited and built, coached by Voights, one of Waldorf's All Americans.

But this kind of loss was worse than anyone imagined it could be. Cal lost its star, Jensen, to a non-contact leg injury early in the second half, and endured two extremely critical and controversial calls by referee Jimmy Cain.

Despite the pain, Cal's rooters considered 1948 a near-perfect football season. Their Golden Bears had beaten USC and Stanford, won every game on the schedule, shared the PCC Championship, then represented the conference well in a postseason contest.

A few days after the Rose Bowl, they packed Harmon Gym, the Berkeley campus' basketball arena. The house was so full, some fans even sat in the rafters as they gathered in tribute to their champions.

Chapter 5

President Robert Sproul spoke first, saying, "By the powers vested in me by the regents of this university, I proclaim this a congratulation and not a consolation meeting. The football team served the student body unusually well. Even before the game, I planned this as a congratulatory meeting. Nothing that happened New Year's Day changed my convictions.

"The Northwestern victory achieved New Year's Day bore the 'Mark of Cain.' "

Chapter 6

REIGN OF THE WALRUS

A ny sensible person would have concluded that Pappy Waldorf's Bears had reached the top of the mountain in 1948.

They'd gone unbeaten in the regular season, and lost the Rose Bowl to Northwestern mostly because superstar Jackie Jensen had gotten injured and — they firmly believed — referee Jimmy Cain had blown two critical calls.

So heading into the 1949 season, things weren't exactly bleak. But it seemed to be a time for realism.

Cal lost four key starters to graduation, and then Jensen met with Waldorf early in the spring because he had been offered $50,000 to sign a pro baseball contract.

Pappy Waldorf advised Jackie to turn pro, since it was too much money to pass up, but said, "Promise me you'll come back to get your degree."

Jensen signed on as an outfielder with the Boston Red Sox, and went on to become American League's most valuable player. Jensen eventually earned his degree and returned as Cal's baseball coach for a time.

But how could anyone replace Jensen?

"Jack was the most unbelievably gifted athlete I've ever seen," said his pal and future partner in an Oakland restaurant, Cal quarterback Boots Erb. "He could do absolutely anything in any sport. When he signed to play baseball, honestly, I think most everyone's expectations for the '49 season dropped a little."

Jack Swaner was expected to take Jensen's place, but he suffered a leg injury during practice before the first game and didn't see action until the season was almost over.

Halfback Billy Main and end John Cunningham were declared ineligible by PCC's revised interpretation of wartime eligibility rules. Center Doug Duncan joined Naval Intelligence. End Norm Pressley missed the first six games because of a leg injury - and the list of the missing grew longer.

However, the situation provided opportunities for new talent to emerge, and Pappy always seemed to have more talent available.

Roy Muehlberger won a varsity spot at left defensive tackle, despite the fact he had played no high school football and only a year with the Ramblers after he transferred from Cal Tech. Making varsity meant he was issued a team traveling jacket - a big deal at that time.

What Muehlberger remembered most about his first road trip to Wisconsin was this: "I got the hell kicked out of me, and it was the first time I ever saw a woman at a football game wearing a sweatshirt and slacks. At Cal, women would be dressed up."

Cal won that game 35-20, but the joy of that victory was dampened by Charley Sarver's knee injury. He had rushed for 88 yards on just six carries, but a Wisconsin defender had been playing dirty. Each time he tackled Charley, he would slam Sarver's head to the grass and punch him in the stomach with both hands.

Finally, Charley had enough.

Cal faked the ball up the middle, Sarver took a pitchout. He saw the defense shift to close off the outside.

"I should've cut back and headed for the goal," Sarver said, "but I wanted to pay that guy back, so I slowed down, thinking he'd try to tackle me. Then I was going to use my knee as a hammer to his head.

"We collided, but in slowing up, I had given the pursuit time to catch up. All these defenders landed on me while I was standing up with my right leg straight. My right knee split open and my leg bent at a 45-degree angle to my body.

"The doctors had to remove my knee ligament and I was in a cast from toe to neck for six weeks. It taught me a hard lesson. There should be no payback in athletics."

Even though he wouldn't be able to play, Charlie's teammates elected him honorary captain for the following Saturday's game against USC. They vowed to get the game ball for Charlie.

The Bears were 4-0 when they hosted mighty Southern

California at Memorial Stadium. Cal had knocked off the Trojans 13-7 in Los Angeles the year before; thus the two schools found themselves locked in a war for supremacy in the old Pacific Coast Conference.

Although no one realized the impact at the time, the 1949 Cal-USC game was the Bears' first to be carried on local television. Waldorf obtained a TV set and had it hooked up behind the Andy Smith Bench on the Cal sideline.

The game was a classic. Cal was crippled by early-season injuries, but quarterback Bob Celeri flashed moments of brilliance to keep the Bears alive.

Eventually, the Trojans went up 10-7 on Frank Gifford's 23-yard field goal in the fourth quarter.

Then Brunk stepped into legend.

Bob McGee's kickoff following the Gifford field goal was deep and headed toward Monachino. Brunk was ready to holler for Monachino to take it when the kick began curving back toward him. Frank caught the ball three yards deep in the end zone.

"Everything after that is like a dream. It's the same for me now as it was then," Brunk said. "I was just plain lucky, to be the person standing there at the time, because it changed my life."

Brunk raced up the middle, where Cal had been trying to return kicks all day without much success. This time, the blocking was picture perfect. All American Rod Franz took out two men and a huge hole opened up.

"My friends and teammates tease me that anybody could have run back that kick," Brunk said, "and they're right. But I'm sure glad it was me who fielded that ball."

Brunk broke clear near midfield and veered right to avoid Gifford, the superstar who became a national hero in pro football, then as a TV sportscaster. Pictures of the kick return show Gifford face down on the turf, the last man between Brunk and lifetime celebrity.

"It was crazy!" Brunk said. "The crowd was so excited, one guy threw a cashmere sweater into the air and lost it. He blames me to this day. I heard that a pregnant lady wet her pants. And my brother hugged Marty Cullom (wife of tackle Jim Cullom) in the middle of the men's rooting section."

"I couldn't keep from smiling that Sunday night," Pappy said, "after I watched movies of the game and evaluated our defense. Seventeen Cal players had made 96 tackles, while 19 USC players made 77 tackles. Another way of looking at it was that 58 Trojans were hit by 96 Bears and 56 Bears were hit by 77 Trojans. In other words, we had far more players in on each defensive play than USC."

When the national rankings were released that week, California was voted the No. 1 team in the country.

Meanwhile, a big change on the Southern California college football scene had begun to take place.

Henry "Red" Sanders was the brilliant new coach at UCLA, a man destined to set the Los Angeles area on its ear. Sanders created football's first attack defense - the forerunner to the blitz schemes seen now in the NFL. He also devised the most explosive form of the Single Wing ever seen, and changed the Bruins' jerseys from navy to sky blue.

Sanders was detached from his players and once said, "I'm too busy coachin' 'em to be courtin' 'em." His practices weren't just tough, they were mean. Red's problem was that he had to win every game, any way possible, whatever the cost.

The first meeting between Pappy Waldorf and Red Sanders occurred in 1949, the beginning of a rivalry that took strange turns.

When scouting the Bruins, Eggs Manske noticed UCLA was coached not only to hit opposing receivers above the pads, which was legal then, but also to smash their helmets, hoping to force a fumble.

Red Sanders, his detractors felt, had no qualms about teaching dirty football.

The first half of that first Waldorf-Sanders matchup ended in a 14-14 tie. Then, on the first play after the second half kickoff, a UCLA pass went directly into the hands of Cal's Forrest Klein, who fell down after his interception on the UCLA 39, probably the most surprised man in the stadium.

Celeri immediately went for the jugular. He whipped a pass to Frank Brunk, who then whirled around to score from the 5-yard line.

Roy Muehlberger will never forget the following kickoff.

"It provided the opportunity for the best tackle I ever made," he said. "It was hot on the field - perfect for football, because heat minimizes injuries. My dad, brothers, and many of my boyhood friends were there.

"UCLA received the ball on about the 10, formed up and came

right up my lane. The ball carrier was a half-step too close to his blockers for open field running. His two blockers double-teamed me. At that instant, I knew I had two tackles.

"I got three. It was the fastest stop I ever made. One of the blockers got up slowly and left the field; the rest of us could not get up. My helmet was gone. I knew if I didn't show some sign of life, they would take me out.

"Little did I know, the guys on the bench were screaming, 'Roy, get up! Roy, get up!'

"I crawled around on all fours looking for my helmet. That was all I could do. The strap also flew off somewhere. It seemed like I spent an eternity looking around for my helmet and strap on my hands and knees. It really isn't too difficult to find a helmet lying on a smooth field of grass. I finally found it, managed to get up, then wander around looking for the strap.

"The whole time, my senses were gradually returning. The coaches would have taken me out of the game, but their attention was directed at the two downed UCLA players. One was finally removed on a stretcher and the other walked off with the help of trainers. Of course, my dad and brothers went out of their minds.

"It sure is great being at the head of someone's parade."

Moments later, Ray Solari recovered a fumble for the Bears. And this time, Celeri stuck with the running game. Thanks to Norm Pressley's blocking, Celeri leaped the final few inches for California's fourth touchdown, making the score 28-14.

UCLA scored in the early moments of the fourth quarter to make it 28-21 with 12 minutes left, but California didn't crack.

They coolly took the ensuing kickoff and started another TD march. They advanced 67 yards in nine plays, with Celeri completing two long passes and Brunk vaulting over from the 2.

The final score was California 35, UCLA 21 - Waldorf's third victory over UCLA in as many tries.

Celeri broke three single-game Cal records that afternoon, completing 12 passes for 214 yards and gaining 225 yards of total offense. For the first time in California's history, a player enjoyed a 200-yard passing day.

Reflecting on the win, Waldorf singled out some unlikely heroes:

"I want to give a big hand to our Ramblers. They worked the UCLA plays against the varsity during practice last week and sharpened us up. I want to express my sincere gratitude to all the boys for their help. Congratulations for a job well done."

The following week, Cal knocked off Washington State, 33-14, but it was an expensive win for Cal. Bob Celeri, while being tackled from behind, injured his right foot.

And there was more scary news. When the team returned to their locker room, everyone discovered one of the student managers was listening to the radio broadcast of the final minutes of Stanford's game with UCLA.

Pappy asked, "You fellows hear the score of the Stanford game?"

"Stanford's ahead 27 to 7 and the game's not over, Coach," someone answered.

That sobered everyone in a hurry because Stanford was two weeks away, but the news gave Pappy fodder for a brief postgame chat with his troops: "We have two more rivers to cross and both rivers are at flood crest. Stay well and take good care of yourselves this week. We're going to need everybody healthy."

The following Saturday, California hosted Oregon. Cal put on a record-shattering performance to win, 41-14, scoring 21 points in a lightning span of just 1:15.

Despite the victory, however, the Bears saw Notre Dame slip past them to the No. 1 spot in the national rankings. But of course, with Stanford waiting, there was no time to worry about such things.

Cal went into the Big Game 9-0, while the Indians were 6-2-1, coming off a 63-0 slaughter of Idaho.

From the standpoint of mass appeal, the 1949 Big Game was the biggest ever played. It was the first time Stanford Stadium was completely sold out. In addition, the game attracted 250 sports writers from across the country, was carried coast-to-coast on the CBS Radio network and was the first Big Game televised in the Bay Area.

It was also Stanford's homecoming.

The two most playful Ramblers, Jim Marinos and Henry Clarke, decided to torpedo Stanford's homecoming parade as a prank.

"We drove to Palo Alto early that morning," Marinos said, "and found all the floats and the vehicles hauling them. We noticed one big truck with a float attached was sitting at the exit of that lot. We figured if no one could move it, the whole lot would be blockaded. So we pulled out the distributor cap and spark plug wires and tossed them into some bushes.

"Then, we noticed one float would still be able to pull out. We walked up to the contraption pulling that float and saw the key was in it. So we started it up and hauled that float eight blocks away.

"But as Henry and I were walking back to our car, some Indian worker bees saw us and began chasing us. We made it to the car and took off, but they were right on our tail and chased us through alleys and side streets. Finally, we lost them.

"We were late getting into the dressing room, though, and the kickoff had been delayed because of us. Zeb Chaney and Hal Grant demanded, 'Where the hell have you been?'

"We told them a bunch of Stanford guys ambushed us and we had to run for it. Zeb was so mad he was almost frothing at the mouth. He was ready to have us indicted. It was a good thing the Ramblers kicked Stanford's ass, Henry and I played well, and most important, Cal won the Big Game. I don't think Zeb ever told Pappy."

The Big Game itself was a scoreless stalemate until late in the first quarter, when Gary Kerkorian tried to break it open with a pass to Ken Rose.

Billy Montagne intercepted the throw at Cal's 20, and thanks to Frank Humpert's block, returned it to the Bears 36.

Three plays later, Cal scored on a 54-yard touchdown pass from Celeri to Monachino. Cal missed the conversion, though; the score was 6-0.

Early in the second quarter, Celeri's pitchout to Don Robison went astray and Russ Pomeroy recovered for the Indians on Cal's 16-yard line. Bob White took a pitchout from Kerkorian and slipped past Dick LemMon for a 16-yard scoring run. Kerkorian's successful PAT attempt put Stanford in front, 7-6, which remained the score at halftime.

Early in the third quarter, Cal mounted a 79-yard drive in 11 plays which ended with Jack Swaner's touchdown plunge. Truck Cullom's PAT was blocked by Bill McColl, so the score became California 12, Stanford 7.

Stanford answered with a 76-yard march in nine plays to take a 14-12 lead with five minutes left in the third quarter, so things definitely had gotten serious.

After the kickoff, Brunk was forced from the game because of an injury. Wes Fry telephoned down to the field and suggested that Monachino be shifted from right halfback to left half.

Then just before the snap on what was to a running play for Monachino, Truck Cullom put his left arm behind him and pointed to indicate to Monachino that he was going to block his man to that side and the halfback should go the opposite way.

Monachino burst off left tackle for 84 yards down to the Stanford 4-yard line. It took two more plays to get the ball into the end zone, with Swaner finally lugging it over.

Years later, Monachino said, "That 84-yard run made me an All-American. I owe it all to Cullom's great block and to Wes Fry for shifting me to left halfback."

Needless to say, the long run also changed the game.

Cal mounted a 67-yard scoring march which continued into the fourth quarter. Swaner scored his third touchdown to make it 26-14, and the day's scoring ended with Cal's 71-yard drive in 10 plays, topped off by Monachino's 1-yard burst.

The final score was 33-14.

Waldorf made sure the press understood just how far his young squad had come that year.

"It shouldn't have been, but it has become a great team," he said. "It really doesn't make sense. You'd think in a tough 10-game schedule, there would have been a crack somewhere along the line.

"Somewhere, something should have happened. But it never did. These kids wouldn't let it happen. They wouldn't crack, nothing perturbed them. Seven times this season, this gang has come from behind. Seven times, mind you. Where can you find something comparable?

"They don't get bothered. For instance, at halftime, I told them Frank Brunk was through with a muscle pull in his leg. I said, 'Gang, I don't know who we'll have in there at left half, but you'll just have to block a little harder.' Damned if they didn't.

"It was the same with Don Robison, just a sophomore, mind you. I didn't know he had bruised his hand badly, early in the game, until just before the finish, when one of the boys told me. Ever see any better kicking than that kid did under pressure?

"And Monachino. Now there's a kid for you. He'll play fullback, right half, or left half. Wes suggested we acquaint him at left half just in case something happened to Brunk. We did, and that little guy is just a helluva football player.

"No, we were not a good team at the start, but these boys learned to run and block. I can honestly say at the start of the season I hadn't the slightest inkling that tonight we'd be heading for the Rose Bowl. It's simply amazing."

Brutus Hamilton stuck his head in the jubilant dressing room and said, "Another year like this, and we can take Mr. Waldorf off probation."

As Pappy tightly hugged the game ball presented to him by co-captains Jim Turner and Rod Franz, Cullom delivered his summation of the afternoon's events: "Let there be no more talk of moral victories. What we did to Stanford this afternoon wasn't moral."

During the weeks before the 1950 Rose Bowl, Cullom told a reporter, "Last year, it was just a matter of getting Jensen past the line of defense. This season, we figure we've got to escort the ball carriers all the way to the goal line, so we're putting out a lot more.

"There's another thing, buddy. There are 27 of us who blew the duke last New Year's. Everybody knows we should have won, and we didn't think we'd get another chance. Now that we're here, to everybody's surprise, including our own, we're not missing the boat."

The 1950 Rose Bowl drew 100,963, the first bowl game with a six-digit attendance figure.

Again, Cal faced a more experienced squad peaking at the right time. This trip, it was Ohio State.

But California, as it turned out, was doomed to another horrific, fourth-quarter breakdown.

The Bears led 7-0 at halftime, courtesy of a long connection from Celeri to Brunk and Monachino's 1-yard smash, but there were indications even then that Ohio State was going to be a handful. In that opening half, OSU had 175 yards and 13 first downs, all on the ground, compared to the Bears' 68 yards total offense and only five first downs.

Early in the third quarter, Celeri tried to hit Brunk with a pass, but Vic Janowicz picked it off and waltzed 36 yards to the Cal 30. Curley Morrison finished the short drive with a 1-yard run to tie the game at 7-7.

Later that quarter, a poor snap contributed to a blocked punt. OSU's Jack Lininger recovered the ball at Cal's 6-yard line. Four plays later, Ohio State scored and Cal was behind, 14-7.

Yet the Bears roared back. Their answering drive was culminated by Celeri's lateral to Monachino, who sprinted 46 yards for a touchdown.

As the game wound into the final two minutes it was still tied 14-14, but Cal was pinned deep in its own end of the field. On fourth down from his 16-yard line, Celeri dropped back to punt from the end zone.

Ozzie Harris' snap was low and the ball came to Celeri ankle high. Celeri couldn't pick it up in time, muffed it, then frantically grabbed the thing on the first bounce and started running to his left.

Several Buckeyes were almost on top of him, so Celeri tried to punt with his left foot. He was only a stride away from his end zone as he launched his kick on a dead run. The ball sliced miserably out of bounds at Cal's 13.

Ohio State chewed up the clock, moved to the 5-yard line and then, on fourth and goal, Ohio State coach Wes Fesler intentionally took a delay of game penalty to stop the clock so that the place-kicking unit could set up.

Jimmy Hague, a rangy 200-pound end, hammered through the point-blank field goal and the Bears had lost another Rose Bowl, 17-14.

"Pappy called us together," Muehlberger said. "He spoke in his deep, self-assured voice and restored our composure. The season was over and, as Pappy pointed out, the biggest loss was that this team was now history.

"We would never again play together. That was hard to swallow. We never met before we played together. We toughened, taught, and cheered for each other, a bunch of nobodies who gave more than they had to become the best there was. Four of us made the College Football Hall of Fame: Pappy, Eggs, Rod Franz and Les Richter."

Two days later, the game film revealed the truth. After reviewing it, Pappy said, "The total advance on Ohio State's three scoring drives was a mere 37 yards. Seventeen points from 37 yards. Oh, brother!

"What a way to lose a game."

No one expected the reception the team got when their plane landed. The Oakland Chamber of Commerce staged a "Welcome Home, California Bears" rally and presented them with the Key to the City, which Brunk was pleased to accept on behalf of the squad.

Celeri went on to play quarterback and wide receiver for NFL's New York Yankees (a team that became the Dallas Texans, then went out of business). Then he went to Canada, where he played minor league football while starting Wilfred Laurier University's football program.

Eventually, Celeri became the top college scout for the Buffalo Bills. Bob was the man who assembled the "Electric Company" that blocked for O.J. Simpson. He also brought Joe Ferguson to the Bills.

So the 1949 season, and the Rose Bowl that followed it, produced unbelievable memories — mostly enjoyable — for Cal's football fathful.

It didn't seem like there would be any way to duplicate such heroics in 1950.

On the other hand...

At first, 1950 was viewed as a rebuilding year, since many of the '49 starting players had graduated. As Carl Van Heuit recalled, "We opened the season with four sophomore tackles on offense and defense, a patchwork offensive line and no idea who would be quarterback."

But this was the season which marked the coming-out party for the magnificent Johnny Olszewski.

Johnny O.

Now here was a running with a style so different from that of the legendary Jensen, yet just as effective. Olszewski was fast but also unbelievably powerful and determined — in other words, a monster.

In the opinion of running backs coach Wes Fry, the secret to Johnny O's success was this: "(He has) a tremendous urge to get to the goal line. He's the most elusive player you'll ever see and has a phenomenal shoulder fake, but he's also equipped with an additional weapon.

"If there's no place else to go, he'll take on the other guy, and he usually doesn't come off second best. When he puts his shoulder into a tackler, he seems to take off, as if some hidden spring uncoils to give him power. "

Pappy, of course, noticed the other side of his new star: "He was just a swell kid - level-headed, modest, refreshing, attentive, hard working and easy to instruct - a great team player and inspirational force.

"You couldn't stack a line against Olszewski. He could go up the middle, off tackle or wide. He was grand on delayed plays and he could pass. When we'd throw out a flanker, he was actually a tailback in a single wing. He proved he had the ability to perform every function of an outstanding tailback."

Johnny O was even tougher than Jackie Jensen. Bill Mais said, "He seemed to be made of wrought iron and had a negative pain threshold."

Olszewski attributed his feats to body control. Johnny was an expert high diver. He had won the Long Beach City Diving Championships and spent his summers as a lifeguard. He also studied ballet in high school and became quite good, but as he recalled, "I was ribbed so much, I quit. But the dancing built up my legs. The diving gave me coordination."

Johnny O's varsity debut was sensational. He gained 111 yards on only eight carries during Cal's 27-9 win over Santa Clara.

Still, it was not a happy day for Pappy; he lost a good friend that afternoon. Sam Barry, USC's basketball coach who would have been in attendance to scout the Golden Bears, suffered a fatal heart attack while walking into Memorial Stadium. Before moving to Southern Cal, Barry had taken Iowa to two Big Ten titles.

Barry was also an assistant football coach to Howard Jones at Iowa and SC and had taken over as head coach at USC after Jones' untimely death just before the 1941 season. That year, Waldorf had supplied Barry with scouting reports, game films and other tips which helped his friend prepare an undermanned Trojan squad to face Notre Dame.

USC played Frank Leahy's unbeaten Fighting Irish off their feet before losing a squeaker, 20-18.

After Cal lost to USC in 1947, Barry had given Waldorf a class tie in USC colors. "Because I like you, Pappy, and it will bring you good luck," Barry said.

Lynn started wearing it to every game he coached and didn't lose a regular season contest for nearly four years.

Upon learning the tragic news, Waldorf sent a print of the game film to Southern Cal coach Jeff Cravath with a note which read, "I deeply regret your loss and that Sam was unable to scout Cal for you. He was a good friend and his work should not be left unfinished. I hope you can make do with the enclosed film."

Though the PCC had an unwritten rule against using game films for scouting purposes, even commissioner Vic Schmidt, who believed in doing everything by the book, did not levy punishment for what was viewed as the fair thing to do.

With their tremendous offensive line and stable of great running backs, the Bears had the best rushing game in the nation. Yet, three games into the season, the quarterback position was still unsettled.

Jim Marinos was a senior and had starred on great teams at San Diego High. However, he had endured nearly four years of frustration at Cal. Although he quarterbacked the Ramblers to torrents of touchdowns, Marinos had played little varsity football and was matched in overall ability by sophomores Brent Ogden and Dick Lee.

Cal's coaches decided to play Ogden and Lee in the first three games, while Marinos rode the bench and played for the Ramblers. This gnawed at him, for he knew in his heart he could do the job.

The fourth game of that season was against USC in Los Angeles, a critical conference matchup. Cal had narrowly edged Pennsylvania, 14-7, but the performance of the two young quarterbacks was not stellar. They combined for only one completion in 11 attempts and were intercepted twice. They just weren't moving the ball club.

In accordance with a custom Waldorf started at Cal, the players met each Wednesday evening after practice, without coaches present, to elect a game captain for that Saturday's contest.

During the meeting, John Ralston and Dick LemMon presented

a persuasive argument for their teammates to vote Jim Marinos as captain against the Trojans, saying, "If we're gonna win this conference, we need a guy who knows what it takes. We're not just talking about knowing the offensive system, but also knowing us as individuals. We need someone who won't rattle and will call the right plays at the right time."

The team was sold, and elected Jim to the captaincy.

Marinos was not at that meeting. After working up a big appetite at practice, he and some other Ramblers had rushed to dinner at the Bears training table. Jim was gorging on Jell-O, ice cream and chocolate cake, while Pappy and the other coaches were eating at another table in the dining hall.

Pete Schabarum and Jim Monachino entered the hall, went to the coaches' table and announced, "Well, Pappy, we made a decision. Jim Marinos has been voted captain for Saturday's game. Jim is going to be our leader at USC."

When they heard the news, all of the coaches - Pappy, Wes Fry, Tessier and Manske, looked as though they'd been whacked on their heads with clubs. They were stunned.

Marinos did not hear the announcement, so he asked someone at the table, "What the hell did they say?"

After their initial shock, Pappy and Wes went over to Marinos and said, "Jim, we got the message. The players have spoken and we'll honor their wish. Now, start thinking about starting that game."

Despite the 100-degree heat in the L.A. Coliseum, Marinos' play-calling was superb. He didn't throw often, but when he did, he completed passes in clutch situations.

Cal held a 13-7 lead, but things began to unravel with 30 seconds left. A pass interference penalty was called against Don Robison, which gave the ball to USC at Cal's 1-yard line.

On first and goal, SC coach Jeff Cravath sent in the play, a handoff to the fullback. But by the time the ball was snapped, Demirjian had forgotten which play had been called, and didn't hand off the ball.

Confused and bewildered, Demirjian tried to run what appeared to be a bootleg, but LemMon nailed him for a nine-yard loss. LemMon later told writers, "I had one of two choices. When I saw Demirjian coming, I thought it was a pass. Then I thought, 'What for? The guy's only got a yard to make.' If it was a pass, I had to fall back. But if it was a run, I had to come up. Brother, I sweated that one until I just said, 'To hell with it, here goes,' and I drove in there. I'd probably be jumping off the closest bridge if that guy had lofted a pass over my head."

Cal won, 13-7.

Carl Van Heuit recalled the sequence of events after that victory. The biggest PCC game of the year was coming up the following Saturday against a Washington team with future pro stars Hugh McElhenny and Don Heinrich in the Husky lineup.

"We were staying at the Biltmore Hotel in Downtown L.A. Later that evening, the players and their wives or girlfriends drifted into the Biltmore Grill. We were joined by a large contingent of Cal fans.

"An impromptu party ensued. These uproarious proceedings continued until about midnight. The coaches discreetly did not attend.

"Normally on a Monday after a hard game, we practiced in light pads. When we showed up for practice that Monday, though, we were advised to dress in full gear. Washington was our next opponent, in Seattle. If they won or tied the game, they would go to the Rose Bowl. Our practice that day was long and grueling. It wasn't until twilight turned into darkness that Pappy called us together.

"In a somber, deep voice, Pappy said to Ed Bartlett, 'Bardo, you were seen having a couple of beers at the Biltmore Grill after the game last Saturday night. I think you ought to run five full laps around this field to get yourself back in shape.'

"Bardo got red in the face, then took off. He'd only gone about five yards when Pappy said, 'Anyone else who had a couple of beers at the Biltmore may join him.'

"The whole damn squad broke into a run and ran the full five laps with Bardo."

Even though the Bears had won 30 straight regular-season games had been to two consecutive Rose Bowls and were ranked sixth in the nation, they went into the Washington game as 3 1/2-point underdogs.

There was also a hubbub when a Seattle-based writer grumbled about Waldorf's method of stashing talent on his Ramblers squad and suggested that these athletes basically were guys who couldn't make the grades to stay eligible for the varsity.

That hit Pappy and his staff very hard.

The writer was way off base. The Ramblers' grades were often better than the general student population. As a matter of fact, Rambler tackle Henry Clarke was pulling straight A's. During that season, Pappy continually reported to the writers that eight Bear starters had come from the Ramblers.

Waldorf told the writers, "The Ramblers are indispensable. I hope to see the day they'll be good enough to schedule teams the caliber of San Jose State and Fresno State.

"I look for any lad with reasonable size, speed and coordination. A boy who possesses those three things can be taught to play football in four stages - a season with the freshmen, spring practice, a season with the Ramblers, then another spring practice."

The Ramblers were not a junior varsity, but rather a ready reserve. One of their earliest coaches was Walt Gordon - a Cal All-American tackle and Hall of Famer. He was Cal's first African-American law school graduate and eventually became governor of the Virgin Islands.

In addition to providing replacements for injured varsity players, the Ramblers emulated Cal's opponents in practices. Gordon's squad mastered every offense used on the Coast so well, Amos Alonzo Stagg once said, "They're impossible to scout. You don't know who'll play for them or what offense they'll use."

The Cal Ramblers were an ideal concept for 1950, the first year two-platoon football flourished. Though free substitution offered boundless strategic possibilities, it also opened a can of worms for many coaches.

Earl "Red" Blaik said, "The platoon system is not for the lazy coach. It takes too much planning and work."

However, that didn't bother Pappy, because he thrived on hard work and extensive planning. By the time the Bears played Washington, Cal football had evolved into the epitome of two-platoon football.

The trail to the Bears' varsity began with their Rambler squad. Pappy took every opportunity to compliment Zeb Chaney's men, calling them the "backbone and heart" of the varsity.

Cal line coach Bob Tessier: "Waldorf doesn't have exceptional material. Waldorf just plain makes material. The folks outside assume we have some sort of deep freeze over here and all we do is open the door and pull out a halfback or guard when we need it. That's stupid.

"Our deep freeze is development, our depth is development. It is a continuous program of practice, play and improvement. Without the Ramblers, we would have no varsity. In fact, it isn't until the Thursday night before a game that the two squads are separated. The Ramblers aren't cannon fodder. They're an ever-present reservoir of talent, gaining experience and polish, then bumping up to the varsity.

"A prime example is Jim Marinos. He's solid now. He can look a top-notch player in the eye, but he was not a natural quarterback. He had to work, study and analyze. Then there's Paul Andrew, defensive end. He didn't even play in high school.

"And 'Little Rollo,' linebacker John Ralston. He weighs only 175 pounds and is too light to stay in there any length of time knocking off 200-pound blockers. But after two years on the Ramblers, Little Rollo came in mighty handy early this season when we were hunting for linebackers. He could really hit, could be used at either corner or in the middle and he put out 100 percent.

"That little brown-haired boy deserves a story and someday he's going to be an outstanding coach. Fellows like 'Little Rollo' are tremendous for the morale of a squad because other Ramblers remember him from two years ago and now they see him, little as he is, as one of the links on the varsity.

"That's development - not deep freeze."

Upon arriving in Seattle, two motorcycle cops and a small delegation from the University of Washington Rally Committee greeted the visitors, but there were also signs that read, "Cal Go Home!" and "Cal, You're Done!"

The police escorted the team's buses as they drove past thousands of college students and fans lining the streets, booing the Golden Bears. Meanwhile, at Seattle's Olympic Hotel and at the Washington Athletic Club, alumni in town for homecoming toasted what they believed was one of the greatest of all Husky teams and drank to their success.

Washington coach Howie Odell's ballclub seemed to have more weapons than the Bears. Don Heinrich was acknowledged as the best passer on the Coast that season and Hugh McElhenny was the West Coast's leading ball carrier, having gained an average of 5.7 yards on his 105 carries.

Even Bob Hope, who had been entertaining U.S. troops in Alaska, had phoned Washington athletic director Harvey Cassill, requesting 70 tickets to the game. Hope was disappointed to learn it took all of Cassill's resourcefulness and clout to find just one ticket for the world-famous comedian.

"We knew the key," Pappy said. "We knew our defense had to be at its best for us to win. Washington had a strong offensive team with fine backs like Hugh McElhenny, Roland Kirkby, Jack Seth, and Bill Earley, and a great passer in Don Heinrich.

"We stressed to our defensive team that Washington would probably have the ball for 13 sequences. If our defensive unit could prevent them from scoring in all but one sequence, we would probably win. If they scored in two or more sequences, our chances of victory were slim.

"The game worked out along those lines. Washington did have the ball for 13 sequences and they scored on just one sequence, although they came close to scoring again."

Washington took a 7-0 lead in the early moments of the second quarter. After Johnny Olszewski returned the ensuing kickoff to the Bears' 37-yard line, Waldorf gathered the offense around him and said, "We're 63 yards from a touchdown that will get us back in the game. Now's the time to show what you can do. And if you're not having fun right now, that's your own fault."

The Bears then began a march capped by Schabarum's lunge over left guard from six yards out. The game was deadlocked at halftime, 7-7.

In the third quarter, Cal forged a 64-yard drive that provided a 14-7 lead. The scoring play was a 26-yard shot from Marinos to Schabarum.

Marinos was superb, nailing seven of nine passes that afternoon, providing Cal with the offensive balance the Bears needed.

Late in the game, Cal was still ahead, 14-7, when Washington mounted a 14-play, 80-yard march to the Bears' 2-yard line. It was fourth and goal from the two and Heinrich tried to throw a backward shovel pass to McElhenny, but Heinrich was pursued by Dwight Ely, and Dick Groger intercepted the toss.

Groger picked off the ball at his 2-yard line and ran it out to Cal's 14. The Bears merely had to hold onto the ball and run the clock out.

On first down, Monachino carried over left guard for six yards, but California was called for an illegal motion penalty and the ball was brought back to the Bears 9. On first and 15, Monachino carried again, but was walloped for a 3-yard loss.

Facing second and 18, Marinos called Monachino's number again. This time, Monachino was smashed by the middle of the Huskies' defensive line and fumbled. The ball was recovered by Washington's Ernie Stein.

Waldorf had just pulled out a new cigar when he saw it all happen. He shouted, "Sonuvabitch!" Then, still holding the cigar and with players gathered around him, Pappy calmly said, "Anybody got a light?"

Monachino remembered it so well.

"Pappy was probably getting ready to burn me at the stake," he said.

But the Bear defense saved the game - and maybe Monachino.

On first and goal at the Bears 9-yard line, McElhenny was nailed by Bob Minahen and Groger for a 6-yard loss. Then, on second and 16, Heinrich tried a jump pass, but Ed Bartlett blew in, pounded Heinrich and caused him to cough up the ball, which was recovered by Minahen to close the deal.

At last.

The following Monday, Pappy told a gathering at San Francisco's Commercial Club just how the Bears were able to pull off their triumph in Seattle.

He said, "I am fortunate to be a coach at a university with unbelievable spirit and tradition. Each and every University of California player feels this. There is no dividing line between the Ramblers and the varsity and there never will be.

"I'd like to tell you about Ozzie Harris. You may remember him as the young man who, unfortunately, made the bad snap that had something to do with Ohio State winning last year's Rose Bowl. When I introduced Ozzie at a campus rally later, he received the biggest hand of all. His mistake had been forgotten. That, in a nutshell, expressed the California spirit. He has proved his worth.

"Of course, there's Carl Van Heuit, our safety. During the Rose Bowl practice of 1948, he impersonated Aschenbrenner of Northwestern. He took such a terrific beating, he was given the Ken Cotton Award as the most courageous player on the squad.

"When we needed to pick a safety last year, we decided on Van Heuit. We realized he was too short and too slow. But he has been there ever since, and he still is too short and too slow. But he has a heart that stretches him to the size of the biggest end.

"Each time we play, I can promise only this. From the last man on the Ramblers to the top man on the coaching staff, California will give its best effort."

When asked about the possibility of playing in Pasadena for the third year in a row, however, Pappy answered, "The Rose Bowl is ages away and someplace over in darkest Africa. Right now, I'm concerned about the overgrown little brothers from Westwood."

A few days before Cal played UCLA, an article appeared in a Los Angeles newspaper denouncing Waldorf as a hypocrite and a general no-good character. In recalling the incident, Pappy added, "Just by coincidence, that L.A. article hung in our dressing room all week. How it got there, I don't know."

Wes Fry felt the basis of Cal's strategy for that important game had to be, first and foremost, "Sticking Olszewski's nose into the line."

Fry's strategy worked to perfection, and the day ended with a 35-0 Cal romp.

Johnny O carried 18 times for 144 yards. Afterward, Fry was elated over the Bears' performance and proclaimed, "It was the most deceptive we've been all year and everything worked like a charm. We used eight running plays and two pass plays going both ways, for the better part of the afternoon. Marinos stuck with those strategies and they were all we needed."

After the game, when a reporter asked Pappy about the following week's opponent, the University of San Francisco Dons, he answered, "USF won't be easy. We'll have trouble."

Cal faced what was probably USF's best team ever. Eleven players from that powerhouse went on to play in the NFL. What could have been a football game for the ages in Memorial Stadium, though, was played under monsoon conditions, and only 14,000 diehard fans showed up.

San Francisco registered the contest's first touchdown in the second quarter. Roy Barni scooped up Don Robison's punt, ran by two Bears as if they were standing still, received a resounding block from Roy Giorgi and raced 84 yards to put the Dons up 7-0.

Soon enough, Dick Groger forced a fumble, which Ray Solari returned for a game-tying touchdown. And for awhile after that, there was nothing to see but rain.

The Bears' turned away a USF threat late in the third quarter, then let Schabarum and Johnny O pound away on a critical drive that saw Marinos somehow find the mud-plattered Olszewski with a pass to the USF 7-yard line.

Pappy's recollection of that drive: "We had the ball on San Francisco's 7-yard line near the right sideline in one of the few fairly firm spots remaining on the field.

"Wes Fry, up in the press box, had noticed that when we stationed a flanker to the wide side of the field, the San Francisco defense moved out toward the middle of the field, leaving the short side — toward the sideline — thinly guarded. He suggested we put a flanker to our left, then run a play wide toward that short sideline with our right end blocking the San Francisco left end.

"These instructions were sent in and everything worked out perfectly. Our right end was able to block the San Francisco end, and Jim Monachino, behind the blocking of Johnny Olszewski, swung around San Francisco's left end and dove into the end zone for the winning touchdown."

After Cal's 13-7 victory, one of the opposing coaches was relieved, the other disappointed.

"Whew, am I glad to get that one over. We were mighty fortunate to win it," Waldorf said.

Meanwhile, USF's Joe Kuharich said, "It was a helluva game to lose. If not for two bad breaks, we might have beat Cal at its own game."

So the Bears had survived yet another regular without a loss, and earned one more chance to present Pappy with his first Rose Bowl victory.

In that '51 Rose Bowl, Waldorf faced an opponent he knew almost nothing about. His scouts had only one opportunity to see Michigan play, and that was a contest performed in the worst blizzard in Big Ten history - heavy snowfall in bitterly cold temperatures with 35 mile-per-hour winds.

In the Wolverines' narrow 9-3 win over Ohio State, Chuck Ortmann punted 24 times, placing 11 out of bounds within Ohio State's 15-yard line. Michigan's center Carl Kreager had, remarkably, made 24 perfect snaps to Ortmann.

The report Pappy received consisted of three lines, "First half - 10 degrees above zero; third quarter - five degrees above zero; fourth quarter - zero!"

Cal's situation worsened when the hugely popular Bob Tessier died unexpectedly of a brain tumor just prior to the Rose Bowl. The loss of Tessier was a devastating blow to the team's morale.

Meanwhile, knowing he lacked the depth to wage an all-out offensive game for 60 minutes, Michigan head coach Bennie Oosterbaan gambled and risked falling behind early. The Wolverines played conservatively throughout the first half.

Because of this, Chuck Ortmann, Don Dufek and Leo Koceski were fresh in the late stages of the contest.

The afternoon's fireworks began early when Schabarum took a pitchout around left end. He outran Ortmann and Tom Johnson to the end zone. Unfortunately, referee Charles W. Brown penalized California for illegal motion, nullifying the touchdown run.

When captain Jim Monachino asked who the offender was, Brown hollered at him, "All of you, goddammit! Now go back and play or get off the field."

Monachino went to the sidelines and reported this to Pappy, who remained calm and said, "Don't worry about that. Just play our game. Keep the pressure on."

It was a scoreless game until early in the second quarter when Ortmann's pass was intercepted by Solari, who made it to the Wolverines' 39-yard line.

Marinos connected with Bob Cummings, who had slipped past Dufek, for a 39-yard touchdown strike. Les Richter's PAT attempt was wide, so it was 6-0.

Late in the second quarter, the Bears had a fourth down and three at Michigan's 4-yard line. Schabarum carried over right guard and saw daylight, but he was betrayed by the slippery football and slid down short of the goal line.

Ortmann and Michigan took advantage of their good fortune, tearing up the Bears with screen passes in the second half. Within those 20 minutes, Ortmann completed 14 of 18 attempts for 145 yards.

Still, Cal held on until Michigan mounted a 15-play, 80-yard march that ended with Dufek's 1-yard scoring plunge and Michigan converted to take a 7-6 lead.

With 1:35 remaining in the game, Cal faced fourth and 12 at its own 13-yard line. Marinos tried a desperation pass, but it was intercepted — setting up yet another touchdown and closing the books on Michigan's 14-6 victory.

After pacing for several minutes to regain his composure, Lynn Waldorf stood before hundreds of sports writers who were present, not so much to chronicle an event, as to conduct an interrogation. They wanted to know how, for the third straight year, his California team had achieved an unbeaten season, but failed to put an end to the Big Ten's reign of tyranny.

"We just got the tar beat out of us in the fourth quarter - period," Waldorf said.

But why?

"You tell me," Pappy said. "I honestly don't know. We have no alibis. There were no injuries to speak of. It's just that we played good ball for a half, fair ball in the third quarter, then came the fourth quarter.

"Why, you ask me, was Michigan's offense so much better in the second half? Maybe the answer is 98 percent Michigan. There wasn't any one play or series of plays you could put your finger on as the turning point."

Each of Pappy's three Rose Bowl losses was different, but there was a theme: Cal led at some point in the second half against Northwestern (1949), Ohio State (1950) and Michigan (1951). Also in each, the Bears were struck with some sort of rotten luck - injury, bad call or weird bounce.

Still, those difficult defeats in Pasadena also showed off Pappy's greatest attributes.

"I learned from Pappy Waldorf how to lose with dignity," said Paul Christopulos, the coach's administrative assistant and arguably the closest man to Pappy through their tenure at Cal. "It is a virtue that many among us sorely lack. Pappy lost three consecutive Rose Bowls, but after each he stood tall and congratulated the winner.

"Pappy went without hesitation into the locker rooms of Northwestern, Ohio State and Michigan to congratulate the coaches and players to whom he'd just lost three heartbreakers. I remember Pappy telling me, 'It's easy to congratulate your opponent when you're the victor, but it takes a lot of inner strength to be the first one to shake the hand of the winner when you're the loser.' "

Chapter 7

TIME FOR CHANGE

Pappy Waldorf's fortunes — at least on the scoreboard — began to decline in the 1950s.

Cal slid slowly from national powerhouse to conference contender to struggling spoiler before Pappy decided he had held the reins long enough and resigned following the 1956 season.

The Walrus had plenty of football left in him, though. He took over as player personnel director and chief scout for the San Francisco 49ers and became an incredibly important ambassador for the fledgling NFL, which was struggling to build relationships with college teams and coaches.

And it's not like Waldorf's Bears fell off the face of the planet after those first magical four years from 1947-51. Pappy's guys had some good years, some big wins and a great record against Stanford.

There was some irony, too, in the fact that Pappy was forced to rebuild the program in the mid-1950s, when his precious depth finally wore thin. But Waldorf obviously did a pretty good job of that, too, since Cal went back to the Rose Bowl following the 1958 season — on the shoulders of a team that Pappy had recruited before he left.

So overall, even when the Bears no longer could produce those long winning streaks or go undefeated seasons, the Waldorf Era was a good time.

Even in the 1950s.

Northern California's finest high school football player of 1951 was Paul Larson, a farmer's son from the Turlock melon patches. Larson was named player of the year that season and five head coaches of major West Coast colleges, including Waldorf, attended his team's football banquet.

It wasn't a difficult choice for Larson, because in those days, Cal-Berkeley was the place for any football player willing to hit the books as hard as he hit a blocking dummy.

Meanwhile, Cal's recruiting efforts had kicked into high gear in the Los Angeles area, too, especially when the school opened a pipeline into the predominantly African-American Jefferson High. No less than 20 Jefferson grads wound up playing various sports in Berkeley.

Cal won its first four games in 1951, thanks largely to the efforts of Les Richter and Johnny Olszewski.

"Richter came to us from Fresno as a fullback," Pappy said. "We didn't have a center, so we made a center out of him. Then we were short a guard, so we made a guard out of him.

"He weighed 237 pounds and had good speed. He was a great linebacker and a great offensive guard — as good as we ever had.

"Because of his speed, we were able to use a new play — '42 Crossfire Wide' — in which the quarterback fakes to the right halfback and hands off to the left half. In the meantime, Richter pulls out, apparently to block the defensive end out and Olszewski comes at the end to block him in.

"Richter would slip the end, the end would be on the ground and Richter and Olszewski would be leading the play all the way down the field. I love that one."

In the meantime, the Bears still owned the Coast and their regular-season unbeaten streak mounted. After a 42-35 win over Washington State, in which Olszewski carried 20 times for a record 269 yards, they'd won 38 in a row when Southern Cal came to Berkeley.

A crowd of 81,490 packed Memorial Stadium, including 6,000 USC rooters who had journeyed northward. USC coach Jess Hill was concerned about the physical condition of his star halfback, Frank Gifford, who had run a high fever only two days before.

On Cal's second play from scrimmage, Olszewski was hit hard and lifted off the ground by a powerful blow from 240-pound linebacker Pat Cannamela. Johnny O apparently landed on his right kneecap and had to be helped off the field. The Bears fullback was really hurting and appeared to be out indefinitely.

"Later, I studied the game film," said future Cal head coach Ray Willsey. "As Pat made the tackle, he caught John around the thigh pads. But when Pat got up, he didn't let go. As he rejoiced in making such a big play, he unintentionally twisted John's leg at the knee. Olszewski lost some of his speed after that hit by Cannamela."

Even without Olszewski, Cal put points on the board. Bill Mais' touchdown shot to Hal Ellis and Bill Powell's run resulted in a 14-0 lead.

But Cal squandered three more opportunities in the second quarter, a bad omen against a team like USC. Olszewski's injury had slowed the Bears offense.

In the third quarter, Olszewski went back into the game. He carried for 30 yards on a trap play, but after being nailed for a loss by Charlie "Tugboat" Ane, Johnny O went down and could go no further.

After a punt, Frank Gifford took a direct snap and cut inside his right end. Ed Bartlett was blocked out of the play and Elmer Willhoite cleared out Richter. Gifford, convoyed by Al Carmichael, slipped past Dick LemMon at the Cal 28 and Ray Willsey at the Bears 10, then scampered in for a touchdown. Gifford's sensational 69-yard run cut the deficit to 14-7.

Early in the fourth quarter, Southern Cal put together a 12-play, 60-yard march to tie the game, with Gifford throwing a touchdown pass to Dean Schneider.

With five minutes left, Johnny Williams managed a 19-yard punt return that brought the Trojans to California's 22-yard line.

Five plays later, on third and goal from the 2, Leon Sellers carried over right guard, spun off a tackler and skidded into the end zone on his belly.

The Bears' regular-season winning streak was over.

As for Gifford, the man who had been burned on Frank Brunk's famous kick return in 1949, the future pro star had a great game, rushing for 115 yards, passing for 49 more, receiving passes for 15 yards and returning kicks for 23 yards — not to mention kicking all three PATs.

Looking back on that game, Cal tackle Bob Karpe said it shouldn't have been surprising that his former Bakersfield High teammate, Frank Gifford, almost single-handedly ended the Bears' streak.

Karpe said, "Frank had a special instinct to do whatever was necessary if you needed a yard, a pass thrown, a pass caught, or a big play. He'd light up whenever it came to, 'Now here's where they separate the men from the boys.' "

The following Monday, Pappy addressed a Cal alumni luncheon at the Commercial Club and said, "I have sipped of a dark, brown, bitter medicine known as defeat. This medicine enables me to distinguish real friends from bandwagon riders and we have found few in the latter category. This medicine also increases the appetite for victory. It brings discernment to the taste.

"But down at the bottom of the vial is the warning skull and crossbones with the words, 'Very dangerous if taken in habit-forming quantities.' "

"That game ended the Waldorf dynasty," Willsey said. "Cal just wasn't the same after that."

However, there was one more big showdown between the Bears and USC. It occurred in 1952, in the L.A. Coliseum.

The game's turning point came early, just four-plus minutes into the first quarter when USC's Jim Sears returned a punt 60 yards for a touchdown and a 7-0 lead.

The Trojans followed with a field goal later in the first quarter to make it 10-0, and no one scored again.

"Late in the game," Bill Mais said, "Olszewski took a pitchout around left end, broke free, then was hit hard by Lindon Crow, the future All-Pro for the New York Giants. Each of them lowered his shoulders, and when they made contact, the collision was deafening. They untangled close to the sideline in front of the USC bench."

Willsey said: "They were like two wounded bulls on their knees, staring each other down, neither willing to give an inch, or show any sign they were hurt. Neither was about to crawl away. Both would have to be carted off."

Later that year, Cal lost to Washington, 22-7, in a game riddled with judgment calls. Olszewski and a few other other seniors, who were never ones to complain, left the field berating the officials.

Jim Hanifan remembered the frustrations of that road trip well.

"When our bus arrived at the airport to take us to our plane home, we learned that the flight was delayed, which ticked us off even more," Hanifan said. "Bill Mais and Olszewski suggested, 'Let's go into this bar and get a beer.' I was 19 years old, definitely not of drinking age, but I tagged along and we took stools at a big oval bar.

"Suddenly, Pappy and the other Cal coaches walked into the place. They walked around the bar and sat down opposite us. I thought to myself, 'Uh, oh. I'm in big trouble now.' Pappy said to the bartender, 'See those young men over there? Get 'em a round of beers on me.' If I hadn't already felt that way, I'd have died for him after that. Pappy understood human emotions.

"Pappy had a tremendous personality. I found myself growing closer to him as the years went by."

Hanifan was struck by how gentle and low-key Waldorf was when he first met him. "He told me, 'You know, you're the first end we've ever recruited. We'd like to have you here,' " Hanifan said.

Hanifan, who ultimately became an NFL coach himself, worked most closely with his end coach, Eggs Manske, and became so influenced by Manske that his teammates called him "Little Eggs."

Meanwhile, Waldorf and Co. were still busy trying to piece teams together. And it was getting tougher each year.

"There were several quarterbacks at Cal's spring practice in 1953," Paul Larson said. "I was a second-string left halfback. Sammy Williams had the inside track at quarterback, but he suffered a broken collarbone.

"Next thing I knew, Pappy wanted to see me. He said, 'Paul, I'm going to ask you a question. I'd like to know what you'd think about doing something, but I don't want you to feel any pressure about how you answer, if you really don't want to do it. It's all up to you and it won't change anything between us.'

"I took a big gulp, then he asked me, 'I want to know if you want to be our quarterback.'

"I told him I would, and that I knew I could do the job. Later, I found out Pappy had asked (assistant coach) Jim Sutherland to pick the quarterback he wanted to work with, and Jim chose me.

"In my first meeting with Sutherland, he told me, 'We have a very simple attack. We go where they ain't.' Years later, Craig Morton told me he did the same thing in the NFL."

With Cal's new passing attack, 1953 turned into a roller coaster year for the Bears. One week,they whipped Washington, 53-25; the next Saturday, they played Oregon to a scoreless tie on a muddy field.

When Pappy tried to explain it, he said, "Things happen sometimes that don't make sense. You ask me why a team can look so bad one week and so good the next. I can't answer because I don't know.

"It's something you can't figure out, not even when you've been around as long as I have. Possibly it was a matter of timing. Offensive football is like a watch, in that it requires delicate adjustment. Little changes can throw it off or make it work. Often a matter of inches can make the difference. By that margin, a key block is made or it isn't and the play succeeds or it doesn't."

Ohio State visited Berkeley on Oct. 3, 1953, for a nationally-televised game. The crowd of 47,000 included Crown Prince Akihito of Japan, newly-appointed Chief Justice Earl Warren and General William Dean. It was also the first on-field meeting between Lynn Waldorf and Woody Hayes.

Hayes' team dominated the game. Cal held a 19-13 lead well into the third quarter, but wound up losing, 33-19 despite Larson's 13-of-25 passing day, good for 170 yards.

Cal's 40-0 rout of Pennsylvania was highlighted by Jerry Drew's magnificent 91-yard touchdown run — the first time he'd ever touched the ball in a varsity game.

California wound up with a 4-4-2 record in 1953, but the future appeared bright because Waldorf had recruited one of the best quarterback prospects he'd ever seen. Ronnie Knox was the nation's most publicized high school football player in 1952.

During the last two weeks of spring training in 1954, each session ended with a scrimmage between a unit quarterbacked by Paul Larson, and coached by Wes Fry, against a squad quarterbacked by Ronnie Knox and coached by Suds Sutherland.

Ronnie performed miserably in those scrimmages, failing to seriously challenge Larson for the starting job. It also became evident that a relationship had formed between Larson and Sutherland. Suds' tutelage would enable Paul to rank among the nation's leading passers for two straight seasons.

Cal opened the 1954 season by hosting No. 1-ranked Oklahoma. The game was a showcase for NBC to kick off its schedule of national telecasts.

The Bears hung tough through the third quarter, but an 82-yard touchdown bomb that broke the Bears backs. Oklahoma went on to win, 27-13.

But Cal's tortuous schedule had only begun. The Bears had to face Ohio State on the road, and by then the Buckeyes had ascended to the No. 1 spot in the national rankings.

The Bears played valiantly, allowed the Bucks past the 50-yard line only three times and gave up only three long gainers, all by Hopalong Cassady. Unfortunately, those three trips past midfield all led to OSU touchdowns and Cal lost, 21-13.

After the game, Larson was walking from the locker room to the team bus, when Woody Hayes approached him. Woody put his arm around Paul, who only minutes before he had described to sports writers as, " ... a mad dog quarterback. It's impossible to figure out what he'll do next."

The Ohio State coach said to Larson, "You're a great quarterback, Paul, and you played a good game. You wanna know how I beat you?"

Larson was interested, and Hayes explained that, of all things, depth had been the difference. Hayes' reasoning was sound, since none of his players went 60 minutes as Cal's stars had — but the situation was ironic because Waldorf's early Bear teams had worn people down exactly the same way.

The following week, Cal jumped to a 13-0 lead against Oregon and then got blown out, 33-13.

After the game, a reporter asked, "If you had it to do all over again, what changes would you have made?"

Pappy obviously hadn't lost his sense of humor He said: "Stay home."

On Oct. 30, Cal hosted the No. 1-ranked and unbeaten UCLA

Bruins, the third time that season the Bears faced the nation's top team. Earlier that season, Red Sanders' wrecking crew had humiliated Stanford, 72-0. Stanford alum Lloyd McGovern witnessed that debacle and recalled, "I became so angry watching Red Sanders' thugs run up the score, I was ready to jump from the rim of the Coliseum into the Olympic swimming pool next to the stadium, just so I'd take the next day's headlines away from the Bruins."

Needless to say, Cal was a huge underdog and, sure enough, the Bears' running game contributed almost nothing that afternoon —28 yards on 28 carries. But Larson was brilliant and added a new definition to the term "iron man." The 175-pounder from Turlock played 60 minutes, completed 25 of 38 passes for 280 yards, punted four times for a 38-yard average and intercepted a Primo Villanueva pass.

Cal lost, 27-6, but afterward, Sanders said, "I don't have adjectives adequate to describe Larson. I don't know how you can stop him. We rushed him hard all the first half, but he always got the ball away."

High praise indeed, for the Bruins went on to an unbeaten 9-0 season that year, were crowned national champions and Sanders was voted coach of the year.

Next Cal hosted Oregon State. Cal built a 12-0 halftime lead on the arm of Paul Larson. Then in the third quarter, Jerry Drew exploded for 118 yards and a touchdown on just three carries.

In the closing minutes of the game, Pappy received word from the press box that Drew was very close to the all-time PCC single-game rushing record, so he told the team to give the ball to Drew. Jerry set a record of 283 yards on 11 carries - a mind-boggling average of 25.7 yards per rush, with 267 of those yards coming in the second half.

Pappy had great affection for Larson, who played so heroically in the face of occasional long odd, and often recounted two incidents in Paul's career.

Larson threw for 1,537 yards in 1954, became the first Cal passer to break the 1500-yard barrier and led the nation in passing. Moreover, Paul was the team's best punter, averaging 34.5 yards per kick. He also led the Bears with eight interceptions and averaged 28.5 yards per kickoff return.

Hanifan caught a Cal-record 44 passes that season for 569 yards and 7 touchdowns.

But things were going backwards for Pappy and California.

Cal was hammered by UCLA the following year, 47-0, as Sanders ran up the score. Cheap shots led to several scuffles.

Afterward, Sanders commented, "That was the weakest California team I've ever seen. They have a few boys who can play football, but that's not enough. I guess they haven't been getting good freshmen for the last two years."

Several weeks later, it was revealed Sanders had obtained bootlegged Cal game films and had used them to prepare for the game in violation of an unwritten PCC rule. Pappy cornered Red at the PCC coaches' meeting and said, "Red, you used films of our games to scout us and I know you did it. You know that's against the gentlemen's agreement the coaches in this league have."

Sanders replied, "Aw hell, Pappy, if I'd known I was breaking a gentlemen's agreement, I wouldn't have done it. I just thought I was breaking a conference rule."

When Pappy, Stanford's Chuck Taylor, Len Casanova of Oregon and other PCC coaches compared notes on Red's ruthlessness, Pappy said, "He makes us look like a bunch of choir boys."

Meanwhile, Oregon's Orlando Hollis embarked on a mission to expose the corruption within Los Angeles' two PCC members and the University of Washington, even if it meant wreaking havoc on their football programs.

Charges and counter-charges were leveled. Finally, PCC commissioner Vic Schmidt demanded that all conference schools open their books and face investigation. When Cal was scrutinized, Zeb Chaney was grilled under oath for eight hours in a session attended by all of the conference's faculty athletic representatives.

During the hearing, it was revealed California had administered a grant-in-aid program that stepped beyond PCC guidelines. Schmidt fined Cal $25,000, which cost Zeb his job.

USC and UCLA, on the other hand, refused to open their books, give any testimony or cooperate in any investigations. In response, the commissioner declared UCLA's players guilty and ineligible until they proved their innocence to him. All of UCLA's sports teams were placed on probation and were ineligible for championships.

USC and Washington also were penalized. The punishment stipulated that none of these three schools could share in Rose Bowl receipts for two years. As a result, three PCC members — UCLA, USC and Washington — were on NCAA probation at the same time. The ludicrous situation eventually led to Schmidt's resignation and the breakup of the Pacific Coast Conference.

Meanwhile, Cal's 1956 season focused on grooming young talent, especially Joe Kapp, a quarterback from Newhall.

"Being a quarterback can ruin you forever," Kapp said. "It's like handing an 19-year-old the keys to an 18-wheeler or the Titanic. The first time I started a game, in Seattle, Pappy saw my knees knocking and my teeth chattering and said to me, 'Joe, I know what's bothering you. It's about calling the plays, isn't it?'

'Now, you've been working with Wes Fry and you know what to do. Just remember, I'll never question any play you call as long as you have a reason for it.'

"That was a lesson I carried throughout my life. Whenever I had to make a decision, I knew I wouldn't have any problems as long as I had a reason for what I did."

As the '56 season drew to a close, the Bears dropped a 14-13 squeaker to a Washington State team coached by Waldorf's former assistant, Jim Sutherland.

Pappy was as gracious as ever in defeat, even though it was the first time in 15 years the Cougars had beaten Cal, and it dumped the Bears to 2-7.

Waldorf complimented Sutherland as a great passing coach, then said, "This was the perfect way to prepare for Stanford. With this one under our belts, we'll be ready to give them a battle."

Moments later, someone told him Stanford had also lost that afternoon. Pappy lit up and said, "Now it'll be like any other Big Game - absolutely wide open."

Unbeknown to anyone except Louise, Pappy had decided even before the 1956 season that 32 years of coaching were enough, and he'd retire after the Big Game. He also knew his announcement would spark speculation about the reason for retiring.

Some media critics and boosters might cite Cal's dwindling recruiting efforts and the fact that other West Coast teams caught up with Waldorf. Others would maintain Pappy was forced out because of declining gate receipts, because in the days before huge revenue from television rights, Cal football had to shoulder the financial burden of all the other student-athletes.

In truth, the coach was merely ending a three-decade race against time. Pappy had spent 32 years devoting every minute of every day in the spring and fall to football, and forsaking simple pleasures. He could no longer ignore the call for leisure, and for the right to enjoy life with Louise.

When he met with the team the night before the Big Game, Pappy said, "I'm also a senior because this will be my last Big Game."

Needless to say, the players were shocked by Pappy's announcement.

Members of the California marching band learned the news upon returning from a dress parade performance at a San Francisco movie premiere. They immediately hopped into cars and raced to Pappy's home on Grizzly Peak Drive to give him a midnight serenade.

Pappy came out on his porch in his nightclothes and spoke to the band with tears welling in his eyes. "This is one of the finest compliments ever paid me," he said. "It is a grand gesture. Your band is the epitome of the University of California. I have always admired your spirit and organization."

Waldorf played it straight in the days to follow, when writers probed for the real reason he decided to retire. He told the press, "I think people get tired of looking at the same old face after a while.

"Before the season, I had decided to leave the University of California. In my statement, I said 'retire' rather than 'resign' because I want to fulfill my obligation. I have worked this year to tidy things up for my successor. We lose only two starters, we have a good bunch of freshmen and I will keep working through spring to get a good frosh team for next season. I believe the University of California will play a competitive part in the Pacific Coast Conference."

Pappy was right; that group of players took Cal to the 1959 Rose Bowl.

And his '56 season wound up with a storybook ending, a 20-18 upset victory over Stanford. Waldorf was carried off the field by his last Cal team.

An emotional crowd of 18,000 massed outside Memorial Stadium for Pappy's final balcony speech. He told those rowdy Cal rooters, who were never shy in their displays of enthusiasm, "Sometimes they say you're rough. Sometimes they say you're vulgar. Sometimes they say you're even barbaric. I don't care. I love you and I always will."

There is no question Pappy Waldorf ranks among the coaching giants in the history of college football. Waldorf posted an astounding record of 173-99-21 at five schools from 1925 through 1956.

That record, however, becomes downright astonishing upon closer inspection. At every one of Pappy's coaching stops - Oklahoma City University, Oklahoma A&M, Kansas State, Northwestern and California - he inherited woebegone programs and won almost immediately. Amazingly, Waldorf's teams captured conference championships everywhere he coached.

Lynn Waldorf was 54 years old when he retired from coaching, and though considered an old man in a young man's game, he still had a lot of living ahead of him. He and Louise looked forward to bird watching, fishing and spending moments with close friends, such as Henry Schacht and his wife.

Schacht had never been involved in football, but was highly accomplished in the field of agriculture. Henry had a farm news radio program and was a contributing editor of Farm Journal magazine. On one occasion, he arranged for Pappy to be a celebrity auctioneer at the sale of a range bull for charity.

After recharging his batteries, Waldorf was ready to embark on a second career. He listened to several propositions, though none involved football. The most attractive was the position of director of public relations for a prominent San Francisco hotel.

Then one evening, while the Schachts were at the Waldorfs for dinner, Pappy told Henry that the 49ers wanted him to take charge charge of their college scouting activities. Henry told Lynn this was great news, and he was happy Waldorf could still be a part of the game.

Pappy, however, didn't seem very enthusiastic about it.

"I'm hesitating as to whether or not to take that job," Waldorf said.

"Why is that?" asked Schacht.

"I've always been associated with the college game," Pappy replied. "I don't know if it would be right to become involved with the pros. I feel I would be turning my back on college football, that it would appear I don't care about my friends in the college game and that none of it meant anything to me."

Henry could see his friend was worried, but he couldn't imagine how Lynn could think being involved in the game he loved could be seen as a betrayal.

"Lynn," he said, "you don't owe college football anything. After all you've done for your players, your fellow coaches and for the schools where you've coached, no one will say you turned your back on college football. If you would enjoy working with the 49ers, then do it. No matter how much we're willing to help others, we still have to take of ourselves."

Henry Schacht's encouragement played a big part in Lynn's decision to join the National Football League. However, if Schacht had possessed intimate knowledge of pro football in the mid-1950s, he might have told his friend to take the hotel job.

Fortunately for all concerned, Waldorf realized he could contribute to the game he loved by being a part of the NFL. Ultimately, he made major contributions to all organized sports.

Pappy's 12-year stint as the 49ers director of college scouting was hardly ceremonial. In fact, Waldorf's influence was absolutely critical, not only to the 49ers, but to the entire NFL at a time when it was struggling not only for recognition, but legitimacy.

The league had precious little prestige in the late 1950s when Pappy came aboard. Most scouting operations were haphazard, and relations between pro teams and major universities had broken down due to questionable deals, signing of college underclassmen and other practices that reflected poorly on the NFL.

Scouts were barred from many university practice fields and stadium press boxes. The situation was dismal.

"What a blessing it was to have Pappy Waldorf join us at that time," said Lou Spadia, then the media relations director and later president of the 49ers. "(Commissioner) Pete Rozelle was delighted Pappy was involved with the league. It was as if Pappy gave us credibility."

Indeed, Waldorf became the NFL's conduit to the American Football Coaches Association. Pappy's friendship with giants of the college game broke down the barriers that had kept the NFL outside the fraternity.

"Pappy knew everybody," Spadia said, "and everybody liked him. There was this great respect for Pappy, so they'd believe him, when someone else might have gotten the door slammed in his face."

When he appeared on campuses to scout, Pappy was often asked by the head coach to tell their squads how to be happy and successful during their life's journeys. Waldorf relished these opportunities to touch young men.

Pappy would tell them, "Playing pro football is fine, but fleeting. It should never be thought of as a path to life's true riches; it's not necessary to have things, but it's urgent to become good at something meaningful and to develop your potential. Don't just think of yourself and always respect others, regardless of their station in life. Your lifetime is the biggest team game you'll ever play."

When Pappy visited the University of Oregon, future All-Pro Dave Wilcox recalled, "It was as if Michael Jordan had arrived on campus."

Waldorf drove Pontiacs, and each year he would arrange to have his old car sold in Berkeley, then ride a train to Detroit to pick up a brand-new Bonneville. Pappy broke in each new auto by driving to Woody Hayes' house near Columbus, where he stayed for six weeks while he observing spring practice at area colleges.

Woody's son, Steve, remembered those visits: "My dad never talked about football at home and never had any books on football in the house, but he kept Pappy's book in his bedroom. He and my dad would talk about the Civil War for hours on end.

"I remember going out to lunch with Pappy once. He ordered a steak cooked one minute on each side. I like my steak rare, but that was too blood red for me."

Pappy received similar hospitality from Frank Gifford. He stayed at Gifford's apartment in New York whenever he was in town on business for the 49ers. It might seem odd that a former coach would be friends with a player from the team that ended his long winning streak, but great competitors are bonded in a way that transcends wins or losses.

Louise would accompany Pappy when he visited the University of Illinois. They stayed with Burt Ingwersen and his wife. In addition to the time Pappy spent eyeballing local football talent, the Ingwersens and Waldorfs would go on bird-watching trips.

Spadia made it clear, however, that Pappy wasn't just a goodwill ambassador. He was a scout, and a darn good one.

Waldorf believed that, given equal height, weight and speed, the most important factors in a pro football prospect were character, smarts and quickness. To Pappy, aside from playoff games, the NFL draft was the most important day of the year. Draft picks were gold.

During the years Waldorf was with the team, the 49ers preferred not to trade their players. If they traded a player, they made sure to receive one or two picks in the next draft.

"He brought the same qualities of organization to our scouting that he'd used to succeed in coaching," Spadia said. "Up to that point, scouting usually involved coaches calling their old cronies and getting information. It was a lot of hearsay and reading magazines. We'd done a few things to make it more professional before Pappy was hired, but he changed things completely.

"He organized our entire scouting program. He hired area scouts, met with them regularly, supervised the whole network and the processing of information. Of course, Pappy knew talent when he saw it. He talked us into drafting a defensive end named Tommy Hart, who everyone thought was too small for the NFL. It turned out Pappy was right. Hart was really quick and became a heck of a pro player."

Did Pappy have drawbacks as a pro scouting director?

"If he did," Spadia said, "it was that he was too honorable for the job. He never did anything secretive, like timing players surreptitiously. He always worked with the schools and got permission for everything.

"Pappy was as competitive in scouting as he had been in coaching, but he always competed fairly. I guess some people would call that a drawback. But they'd be wrong."

Waldorf's contributions to the National Football League were recognized when the 49ers held a retirement party for Pappy on Oct. 6, 1972, at San Francisco's Fairmont Hotel. Pete Rozelle took the opportunity to personally thank the greatest spokesman his league ever had.

Coincidentally, Woody Hayes and his Buckeyes were in town for a game against Cal the following day. Woody actually left his team to attend the Waldorf party.

Hayes said, "I want to say a few words about the greatest man in the world. For Pappy, nothing could keep me away."

Chapter 8

THE BIG GAME

Nothing means more to Cal football loyalists than a win over Stanford.

Winning seasons are gratifying, bowl appearances might be special, but triumph in the Big Game — and possession of the infamous Stanford Axe, a trophy which dates back to 1899 — transcends all other accomplishments. As an Old Blue once said, "We've got to remember that beating Stanford isn't life or death. It's much more important than that."

"The only rivalry in all of football that even comes close is the Bears against the Packers," said Cal All-American and former Chicago Bears tackle Ted Albrecht. "At the '75 Big Game, we were sitting in the quonset hut where Stanford's visiting teams dress. Mike White, who I really enjoyed playing for, spoke to us and said, 'Let's just go out and tar and feather 'em!'

"I was so excited running out onto the field, that around midfield, I jumped up and when I came down, I rolled my ankle. I went over to our trainer, who told me in his Texas drawl, 'Boy, don't be comin' to me with any problem now.'

"When I told him I rolled my ankle, he said, 'We'll tape an aspirin to it and you'll be fine.' It wasn't a serious injury, so he taped me and I was all right.

"We won, 48-15, the most points ever scored by Cal in the Big Game. When it was over, we carried Mike White on our shoulders over to our student section. Someone gave him a microphone and he led everyone in cheers. It was a great day because we beat Stanford and we'd had a great season (8-3 and conference co-champions)."

Albrecht helped put the Big Game in context. It was almost everything.

And no Cal coach ever dominated the Big Game like Pappy Waldorf, who lost to Stanford just once in 10 seasons.

After Pappy said he was retiring, he won his last Big Game. Then a year later, Stanford coach Chuck Taylor imitated his old friend, announcing his retiring and firing up his players for a 14-12 victory.

Wild things have happened regularly in this rivalry, including what is undoubtedly the most spectacular play in college football history — Cal's five-lateral touchdown on a kick return with no time left in 1982.

As the Big Games played out during the Waldorf Years, most were exciting wars that produced some of the best moments in the series.

They were thrillers right from the start.

Chapter 8

In 1947, Pappy's first year in Berkeley, Cal was a huge favorite but needed a near-miracle to win. Paul Keckley, a 160-pound left halfback from Pomona, had been out of action for a few games because of an injured shoulder, and had been listed as out for the Big Game.

As game time approached, though, the shoulder looked better and it was decided Keckley might see limited action.

The Cal team stayed at Ghirardelli's Chocolate Ranch in Palo Alto the night before the game, but it was hardly relaxing. Dinner was to be served at 6:30, but didn't arrive until 9. The evening's entertainment was supposed to be old movies of previous Big Games, but the films were so frayed and jittery, they were difficult to watch, so the players walked out.

Palo Alto experienced an early nip of winter that Friday night and the rooms were so cold, some of the Bears broke up furniture and used it for firewood.

Stanford had not won a game all year and went in as a 40-point underdog, but thanks to George Quist's hard running and great linebacker play, Stanford led 18-14 with three minutes left.

It was only because of George Fong's stamina that California hadn't succumbed by the fourth quarter. He was Cal's stoutest player that day. Time after time, he cut down Indian ball carriers when a missed tackle would have meant a touchdown. Again and again, Fong got a finger or a hand in the way of a Stanford pass.

With time running out, Keckley went up to Waldorf and said, "Let me in, coach, I can play."

Pappy first wanted to talk the team doctor about Keckley's

shoulder, but before he could do anything, Keckley entered the game on his own.

Two plays later, Cal called for a halfback pass, with Keckley breaking back against the flow. Jackie Jensen rolled to the right, then unloaded a wobbly pass that was somehow completed.

Keckley caught the ball around his ankles on the Bears 35, made stumbling progress that caused Stanford's Don Fix to fly past him, held his feet and kept going. Bobby Dodds cleared Dick Flatland out of the way at Stanford's 40-yard line.

Kendall Peck closed in on Keckley around the Stanford 35, but Keckley juked Peck into taking a step in the wrong direction, and that was it.

Keckley romped into the end zone to complete the 80-yard scoring play and Cal survived, 21-18.

After the Cal players returned to their locker room, Pappy addressed them: "Boys, I just want to express my sincere appreciation for the support you have given me this season. You are the greatest bunch of kids I have been associated with in my 23 years of coaching.

"Those of you who will not be with us next year will always remember this game. You should have learned one lesson, and I don't want to sound like *Ladies' Home Journal*, but you should never underestimate an opponent."

Suddenly, Truck Cullom piped up, "Too bad you're not a hundred pounds lighter, Pappy. We would have carried you off the field."

Waldorf summarized the crazy afternoon for the media, saying, "Now I really know what the Big Game means."

Cal went into the 1948 Big Game as a 22-point favorite and needed less than five minutes to execute an 11-play, 59-yard touchdown drive that resulted in Jack Swaner's 2-yard scoring burst to take the lead, 7-0.

This was a Bear team that was undefeated and headed to the Rose Bowl, so most fans assumed that the rout was on after that quick score.

Not necessarily.

Jensen's third-quarter fumble set up Stanford on Cal's 22 and three plays later, Tom Shaw connected with Ken Rose on an 11-yard TD pass.

Truck Cullom slipped through a gap and blocked the conversion kick. It shouldn't have been the game-clincher, but it was as Cal could do no better than holding on for dear life — and that 7-6 victory.

California finally restored order with a 33-14 triumph in the '49 Big Game, but in 1950, serious tension returned.

Pete Schabarum's 31-yard touchdown run put the Bears up 7-0 this time around, but Stanford fought back for the tie despite miserable weather conditions that plagued passer Gary Kerkorian.

Stanford actually had a legitimate chance to win the game at the end, marching from its own 11-yard line to the Cal 27, where two desperation passes fell incomplete.

Nonetheless, the Indians got a tie, which considerably dampened Cal's enthusiasm for a third straight Rose Bowl trip.

For the first time during Cal's Waldorf years, the Bay Area's bragging rights would have to be shared, though Cal retained actual possession of the The Axe. This was also Marchy Schwartz' last game as Stanford's head coach.

After the game, Waldorf said to the writers, "I'm not happy with a tie, but it's no disgrace. Stanford is, by far, the best team we've met all year. They must have completed a million passes."

Schwartz was replaced by Chuck Taylor, who became as close a friend of Pappy's as Marchy had been.

And promptly, the roles of the two teams were reversed.

Stanford went into the 1951 Big Game undefeated and apparently headed to the Rose Bowl. But at the end of the day, Les Richter stood in the middle of Cal's dressing room, game ball clasped to his naked, mud-streaked chest, an unlit cigar in his mouth and another in his hand.

The stogies were symbols of victory. The Bears had scorched the Indians in a 20-7 shocker.

Richter was joined by Dick LemMon, who had made a touchdown-saving deflection of a pass to Stanford's great end Bill McColl.

The upset had been the product of Cal's halfbacks — John Pappa (two scores), Don Robison and Bill Powell — plus Bill Mais' savvy signal-calling. Years later, though, Stanford's Wes Wedge said, "The guy who tore us up and ruined our unbeaten season was Les Richter."

The highlight of the 1952 Big Game was Johnny Olszewski carrying the ball 25 times for 122 yards in Cal's 26-0 victory. In the process, he set an all-time PCC career rushing mark of 2,504 yards.

"I had it in the back of my head," said Cal quarterback Ray Willsey, "that he needed 118 yards to break the record, and I calculated he had 75 at the half.

"All of us were determined Johnny was going to get the mark if it was possible, and toward the end, I heard from the press box that Johnny needed only 28 more. That's when we all pulled together to get it for Johnny, and in our last two possessions I called his number 11 straight times. Next to winning the game, that was the nicest part of the whole day."

The 1953 Big Game was a duel between a couple of great two-way players — Stanford's Bobby Garrett and Cal's Paul Larson. They intercepted each other in a scoreless first quarter, then Garrett threw a touchdown pass to Sam Morley to tie the game at 7 at halftime.

Late in the third quarter, Garrett intercepted Larson for a second time and returned this one 56 yards to give the Indians a 21-7 lead.

Larson scored on an 18-yard run just before the end of the third quarter, then Al Talley galloped into the end zone for a touchdown in the fourth quarter to tie the game at 21-21.

On Stanford's next possession, Larson intercepted Garrett a second time and had a chance to break the deadlock with 1:15 left by kicking a 34-yard field goal.

Unfortunately, Paul didn't have the correct kicking tee. The crowd was so loud, he had to wave to the sidelines, and when the correct tee was thrown to him, Cal was penalized 15 yards for coaching from the sidelines — by the same Jimmy Cain who was such a controversial figure as referee of the 1949 Rose Bowl.

Sadly, it was Larson — for all his heroics — who wound up blaming himself for Cal's inability to win. Larson missed a 26-yard field goal with just five seconds remaining.

The 1954 Big Game saw Cal open a 28-0 lead, then hang on for a 28-20 win, but it was a rough afternoon for Larson.

"The first time we had the ball," said Paul, "I got dumped three times in a row trying to pass, and all these Stanford guys are calling me names as I'm getting shoved out of bounds.

"I found out later from my old high school teammate, Dick Monteith, that Chuck Taylor told his players, 'I want everybody to harass Larson every play. Hassle him all day long.'

"Dick went up to him after that meeting and said, 'Coach, you're wrong about Paul. The more you get on him, the harder he'll play.'

"Well, anyway, they're really workin' me. Finally, I put the ball behind my back and told the referee, 'I'm not giving you the ball back until you start paying attention to what's going on.'"

Waldorf finally lost to Stanford in 1955, then went out in that blaze of glory a year later with his 20-18 upset.

The final victory was vintage Pappy, too, since he changed Cal's blocking assignments completely, showing Stanford something the Bears hadn't done all year.

Waldorf knew Stanford's linebackers would key on Cal's guards, so he had right guard Don Piestrup pull to the right and left guard Don Gilkey pull to the left. Center Frank Mattrocci took the man over him in the direction of the defender's charge and Joe Kapp ran several successful quarterback sneaks.

Cal scored on its first two possessions — in part because the Stanford defense was confused and on its heels — and held on for the win.

Pappy's last Big Game thus became a tribute to his coaching, because his team was so fundamentally sound, he was able to change his entire offense in a few days.

It was a fitting end to Waldorf's coaching career and, of course, another story to add to the Big Game legend.

Chapter 9

THE FAMILY TREE

The coach is gone, but not forgotten.

Pappy Waldorf has been immortalized with a bronze statue in Faculty Glade at the University of California, as well as having a room in the Faculty Club named for him.

Many of his boys went into coaching. They started with his fundamental principles of organization and preparation, contributed their own ideas to this evolving body of knowledge, encouraged the input of young coaches and made Waldorf's philosophy the dominant view of football.

Over half the head coaches in the NFL are philosophically linked to what might be called the Waldorf school of football.

Jim Sutherland was the first Waldorf disciple to achieve national acclaim with a win-with-risk passing attack. The eight seasons Sutherland spent as Washington State's head coach made him one of the winningest coaches in school history.

In his first year at the helm, 1956, Sutherland's squad broke the

PCC's all-time season passing yardage record, and the fireworks were just beginning. Washington State opened its 1957 season by strafing Nebraska for four touchdown passes in a 34-12 road win. The Cougars missed out on a Rose Bowl bid that year by only the margin of a missed extra point against Oregon.

Though never blessed with a true blue-chip quarterback while at WSU, Sutherland still made the forward pass the Cougars' trademark. He and his star receiver Hugh Campbell graced the cover of *Coach And Athlete* magazine.

Campbell later coached the CFL's Edmonton Eskimos to five straight Grey Cup Championships, then became head coach of the Houston Oilers.

John Ralston — the guy his Cal teammates once called "Little Rollo" — also has walked in the footsteps of his mentor. Ralston turned out future All-Pros at Utah State, Stanford and San Jose State.

Here's irony: Ralston is also the only Stanford coach to win two straight Rose Bowls. John has been voted Stanford's football coach of the century. In addition, he was the head coach of two pro teams - the Denver Broncos and the USFL's Oakland Invaders.

In both cases, Ralston did a marvelous job of producing winners from scratch.

While he was at Stanford, Ralston's staff included Dick Vermeil, Mike White, Jim Mora and Bill Walsh — each of whom brought a special style to the NFL. At one time, Walsh spent three years as an assistant at Cal. He is best known as the creator of the West Coast Offense. At present, 14 of Walsh's disciples are head coaches in the NFL or college ranks.

Walsh currently is the 49ers general manager. His head coach is Steve Mariucci, who was the Cal coach in 1995.

Vermeil is the head coach of the St. Louis Rams and his staff includes former Waldorf players Jim Hanifan and Mike White. He also enlisted Ralston's services on a consulting basis for the NFL draft.

Jim Mora led the Philadelphia/Baltimore Stars to berths in all three of the USFL's championship games, then took the New Orleans Saints to their only playoff appearances. He's presently the head coach of the Indianapolis Colts.

Though now retired from coaching, Ralston works tirelessly to promote football. In addition to his work for the Rams, he's a special consultant to the athletic director at San Jose State. Ralston believes football shouldn't be played only by Americans, a view shared by Ray Willsey — a former quarterback for Pappy, head coach at Cal from 1964-71, assistant coach with the Raiders and then director of football operations for the NFL's World League.

Ralston takes the view a step further, however, because he dreams of the day that American football will be an Olympic sport, and is working hard to make that dream a reality.

Mike Giddings played for Waldorf in the early 1950s, then went on to become a linebacker coach for the 49ers and the Broncos. While at Denver, Mike became the first director of pro personnel in the history of pro football. He and his son own Pro Scout, Inc., and for over 20 years have served as consultants to 14 NFL teams.

Jerry Frei is the only man to have played against both Waldorf's Northwestern and Cal teams. Jerry was a guard at Wisconsin in 1942 and then, after serving in the Army Air Corps during WWII, he played for the Badgers in 1946 and 1947.

Frei went into coaching and was Oregon's head coach for five seasons. His former Oregon players include Ahmad Rashad and Dan Fouts. Frei then became John Ralston's offensive line coach with the Denver Broncos and began a long-time relationship with that pro team.

Steve Mariucci was succeeded at Cal by Tom Holmoe. Holmoe played at Brigham Young University, then earned four Super Bowl rings playing and coaching for the 49ers.

Waldorf's presence is always with Holmoe — Bill Dutton, who played for Pappy, and Ed White, former Cal player and Minnesota Viking teammate of Joe Kapp, became a part of Cal's coaching staff.

With Paul Christopulos' help, Bill Walsh and Mike White recruited the quarterback who became the first Cal passer to throw for over 2,000 yards in one season - Craig Morton, a glass blower's son from Campbell, California.

Morton went on to star for Dallas and Denver in the NFL, and quarterbacked the Broncos in their first-ever Super Bowl appearance following the 1977 season.

UCLA is tied to the Waldorf legacy through their legendary track coach, Jim Bush. Pappy hired Bush to assist the Bears' freshman coach, Hal Grant.

Bush was the first Cal grad without football experience to be part of Waldorf's coaching staff. Bush says, "The year I spent working for Pappy provided the foundation for my coaching philosophy. The first priority is to be organized.

"Also, the coach's number one concern, way ahead of their won-loss record, is giving their athletes what they need. The coach should enhance their abilities, help them achieve their goals, be true to them, level with them, be there for them and envision what they'll look like when they're 40 years old. Coaches don't make athletes, athletes make coaches."

Bush is a physical conditioning guru who developed the revolutionary concept of running hills, which involves running uphill for 150 yards, but not at full speed until the last 10 yards. The purpose of this exercise is for athletes to gain their natural stride, develop a forward lean, coordinate the pumping of their arms with the raising of their knees, strengthen their hamstrings, build more muscle fiber, enhance their body control and increase their endurance.

Bush's techniques were so successful, he was asked by the Los Angeles Dodgers and Los Angeles Lakers to work with their athletes. UCLA football coach Terry Donahue added Jim to his Bruins' coaching staff.

Jim Bush is the only man to earn a Super Bowl ring and a Rose Bowl ring in the same season. This remarkable achievement occurred in 1983 — the greatest year in Los Angeles football history. UCLA won the Rose Bowl and the Raiders won the Super Bowl. Bush was on the staff of both organizations at the time.

Division II football powerhouse Cal-Davis also has strong ties to Waldorf. Tom Dutton, the school's vice chancellor, played for Pappy, as did John Pappa. For many years, Pappa was a big part of the UC-Davis football program.

Pappa mentored Mike Bellotti, the head coach at Oregon, and Paul Hackett, the head coach at USC. Hackett, a brilliant offensive mind, has added an innovation to the West Coast offense's play book - the "Trap Pass."

Dean Griffing, who was something of reformed bad boy on Waldorf's one team at Kansas State, went on to a Hall of Fame career in the Canadian Football League, starring for the Saskatchewan Rough Riders, while four of his 1934 Kansas State teammates were drafted by NFL teams.

When the American Football League began, Dean was hired as the first general manager of the Denver Broncos.

Waldorf is still linked to Kansas State, since Ron Hudson, son of Cal's legendary rugby coach Doc Hudson, is K-State's quarterback coach. Doc Hudson had several of Pappy's football players on his rugby squads.

After playing for the Bears, Ron worked as an assistant coach for Ray Willsey at Cal, John Ralston at Stanford, then Mike White at both Cal and Illinois before taking a coaching position under Bill Snyder.

Maurice "Red" Elder, Waldorf's fleet-footed Kansas State halfback, went on to play in the 1937 East-West Shrine Game. Fifty-seven years later, Red's grandson, Jeff Garcia, played in the 1994 renewal of the East-West Classic. It is the only time that a grandfather and a grandson have played in the same all-star contest.

Ralston, who was Jeff's coach at San Jose State, was also coach of the West squad in that game.

In 1998, Garcia quarterbacked Calgary to the CFL's Grey Cup Championship, winning the game for the Stampeders on the last play. Jeff then signed a two-year contract to play quarterback for the San Francisco 49ers.

After San Jose State, Ron Turner was the Chicago Bears' offensive coordinator for four years before becoming the head coach at the University of Illinois.

Illinois, surprisingly, is another football program linked to the Waldorf legacy. Pete Elliott, Waldorf's successor, went on to become Illinois' head man after he led Cal to the 1959 Rose Bowl. His staff at Champaign included Pappy's former player, Jack Hart, and the man who nicknamed Lynn "Pappy" — legendary line coach Burt Ingwersen.

Illinois won the 1964 Rose Bowl, and Pappy drafted two players from that team, defensive back George Donnelly and end Gregg Schumacher, for the 49ers.

Mike White was hired as Illinois' coach in 1980. While there, he took the Fighting Illini to the 1984 Rose Bowl, their last New Year's Day appearance in Pasadena of the 20th century.

These coaches, scouts and administrators represent just the tip of the Waldorf iceberg, but their impact all over the map and over such a long period of time helps put Pappy's influence in perspective.

Certainly these men offer more proof of what Pappy meant to football, and to the people he met while coaching the game.

Back to the spring of 1999.

The party at Dick Erickson's home in the hills of El Cerrito rumbles and the fellows are picking up steam. Brunk has recounted the kickoff return against USC one more time, with color commentary from Boots Erb, who watched it with Pappy on TV. Murakowski's phantom fumble has been cussed and discussed. More than a half-century after the fact, these Bears are still just as livid at ref Jimmy Cain — and still absolutely positive they were robbed of a Rose Bowl victory.

It's amazing, it's fun.

And it's a testament to Waldorf, who tied it all together and helped fashion everyone's future. These, after all, are the men and women who have kept the legacy of Pappy Waldorf alive through the Pappy's Boys organization, through scholarship fund-raisers, through annual reunions, through their drive to have Pappy's statue placed on campus.

They still love the coach, and feel lucky to have shared his company.

No doubt they enjoyed a very fitting poem by Gerald Lubenow as read at their 1997 get-together by University of California Chancellor Robert M. Berdahl:

"Now the Bears were two and seven in the fall of '46 Eight years without a winning team, the coach had hit the bricks

The axe had gone to Stanford, an embarrassing defeat

Led Cal's most loyal rooters to deconstruct their seats.

"Then in stepped Pappy Waldorf, a jolly rotund man

Who shrugged off Cal's inclement past and calmly laid his plans.

Chapter 9

The Bears were not a team, he said, to lose without a peep

But restless, angry giants who had fallen fast asleep.

"Pappy roused Cal from it torpor and shook it to its core

He built a team on veterans returning from the war.

He launched a golden decade, an era halcyon. And when the dust had settled, and Pappy's work was done

That wrecking crew of '47 finished nine and one.

"In '48, the team was great, the best that Cal had seen.

A Golden Boy would lead the way, fulfilling Pappy's dream.

The axe came home on Jackie's runs, the Bears would never lose

Except at year end when they found a thorn came with the rose.

"Through '49 and '50, the unbeaten string would grow.

Monachino and Schabarum and the storied Johnny O

Beat Bruin, Duck and Husky, and the dreaded USC

As Brunk scored on a kickoff and the fans went mad with glee.

"The teams of Waldorf's era will live on in memory.

They were among the finest that Bear fans will ever see.

But Pappy means much more to Cal than storied college joys.

His caring and his decency live on above the noise

Of cheering crowds gone quiet now, he gave us Pappy's Boys."

Afterword

Pappy Waldorf coached during a time when Saturday was the day shoppers crowded stores, the afternoon was meant for leisure and the biggest football games were played. The college game was king and Sundays were meant for church.

In the fast-paced, high-tech times of the modern world many people make football's acquaintance through the National Football League.

Pappy Waldorf's methods of organization and coaching theories changed the face of both college and professional football. His students have shared, and will continue to share, this body of knowledge with aspiring coaches at every level of the game. The Waldorf school of football, with its focus on fundamentals, has provided ample opportunities for its students to make their own contributions. This river of Pappy's gridiron know-how will continue to flow for as long as the pigskin game is played.

Because of his contributions to the National Football League - and to the coaching profession overall - his is a living legacy. It is not a sports tale of long ago and far away, but rather a prologue to what football is today and what it will become in the future. Each January, when the eyes of the world are watching the Super Bowl, the ethos of Lynn "Pappy" Waldorf will always be on display. For, to know Pappy is to know football — and to know the American Spirit.

— John Greenburg

Photo Credits

Courtesy Lloyd McGovern
Foreword, page 17

Courtesy Boots Erb
Insert, page 14 (top)

Courtesy Jan Erickson
Insert, page 14 (bottom)

Courtesy John Greenburg
Insert, page 3 (top), 4 (bottom)

Photos by Ed Kirwan
Insert, page 6, 7, 8, 9, 10, 11, 12, 13 (bottom)

Courtesy Roy Muehlberger
Insert, page 5 (bottom)

Courtesy Mary Louise Osborne
Insert, page 1, 2 (top left), 4 (top right), 5 (top)

Courtesy Carolyn Pickering
Insert, page 2 (top right, bottom left and right), 3 (bottom), 4 (top left), 15

Courtesy San Jose State University (taken by Ron Fried)
Insert, page 16

Courtesy Tournament of Roses Archives
Insert, page 13 (top)